Jazz Treasures
FOR SOLO GUITAR

ISBN 0-634-08989-7

HAL•LEONARD®
CORPORATION

7777 W. BLUEMOUND RD. P.O. BOX 13819 MILWAUKEE, WI 53213

Visit Hal Leonard Online at
www.halleonard.com

PREFACE

The thirty-five challenging chord melody arrangements in this book come from some of the finest composers of the 20th century, and are well-known by musicians and singers. The knowledge in this book is a result of my forty-five years of playing and my arranging of more than two thousand songs for solo guitar. Playing these arrangements will show you new chords, the logic of bass lines, and inner moving voices in chord progressions.

I'm often asked how many songs are played on an average job. The answer, of course, depends on how long one would be playing. As it takes only two to three minutes to play an arrangement, I'd figure twenty songs an hour would be average. It is important to play in tempo. If a chord is too difficult to play, being an arrangement, use an easier voicing or even a single note if needed. As you'll want to connect with your audience, play a variety of familiar songs. For example, standards, contemporary, bossa novas, blues, and Broadway songs all can be arranged for solo guitar. And, the larger your repertoire, the more you are worth. It's a great job to be paid for playing music with the instrument that you love.

This is my fifth book for Hal Leonard. I have received many thank you letters from guitarists world-wide, including jazz guitar majors who have played my arrangements as part of their degree program. It gives me great joy to know that I've helped others as I've always been a caring teacher who is willing to share everything I know. But I also believe that students should study with more than one teacher, given the different approaches and styles of music open to the guitar. A good teacher can improve your playing and strengthen your weaknesses. And, as there is always something new to learn, a dedicated musician is really a student for life. The joy is endless.

—Robert B. Yelin

DEDICATION

I met guitarist Michael Coppola in 1987, when I was living in Norwalk, Connecticut. I played "I Should Care," one of my most difficult arrangements, for him. Michael then played for me his version on his 9-string guitar and my jaw fell open. He had ingeniously expanded the harmonies of the guitar by copying the tight voicings of the piano, an arrangement style of Johnny Smith, who used long finger stretches to reproduce this sound. Michael studied classical guitar in Austria, jazz and harmony in the United States, and continues to challenge himself by playing a wide variety of musical styles. His repertoire includes such artists as Chopin, Mozart, Hendrix, Jelly Roll Morton, the Beatles, and Django Reinhardt. His dedication is why I dedicate this book to him. Michael, who plays with his fingers, is a prolific jazz guitarist who writes charts for his own band and has ten incredible albums to his credit. For more information visit his website at: **www.9string.com**

A special thanks to Johnny Smith, Jeff Schroedl and Jeff Arnold.

CONTENTS

All the Things You Are

Lyrics by Oscar Hammerstein II
Music by Jerome Kern

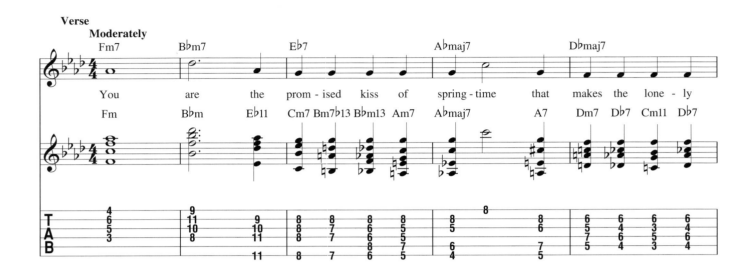

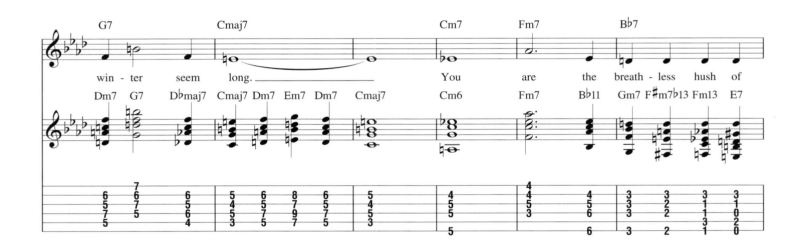

Always

Words and Music by Irving Berlin

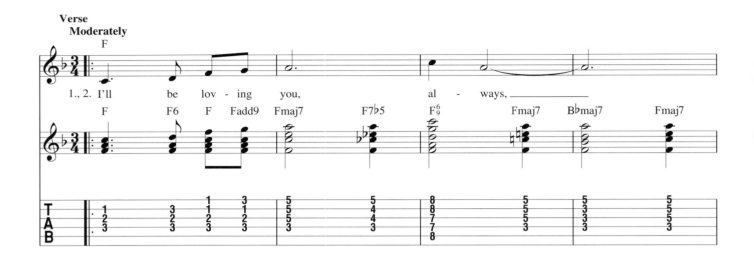

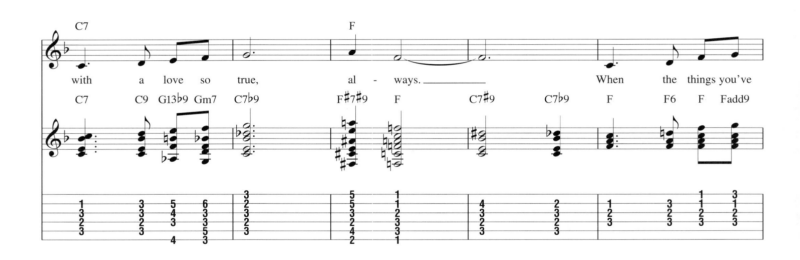

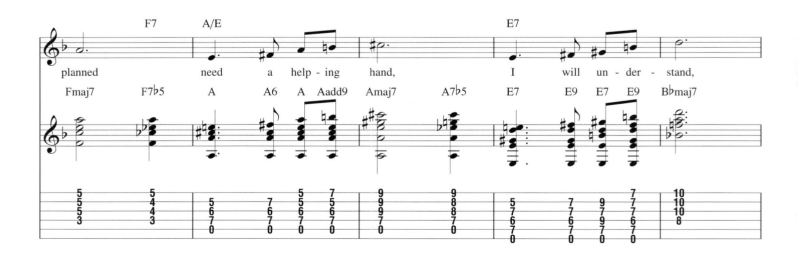

Bésame Mucho
(Kiss Me Much)

Music and Spanish Words by Consuelo Velazquez
English Words by Sunny Skylar

Additional Lyrics

2. Dearest one, if you should leave me,
   Each little dream would take wing and my life would be through.
   Bésame mucho.
   Love me forever and make all my dreams come true.

Bluesette

Words by Norman Gimbel
Music by Jean Thielemans

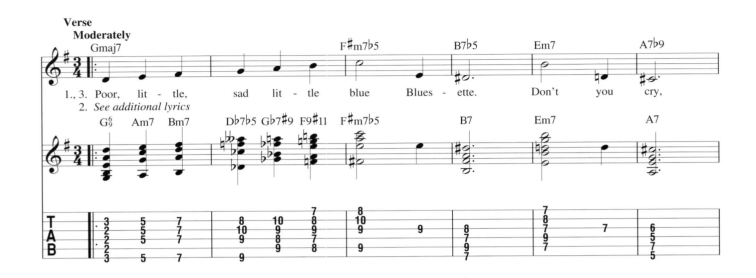

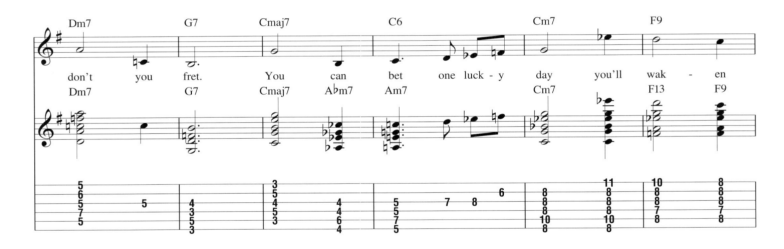

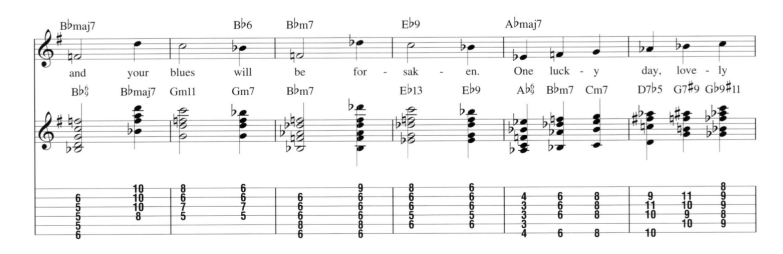

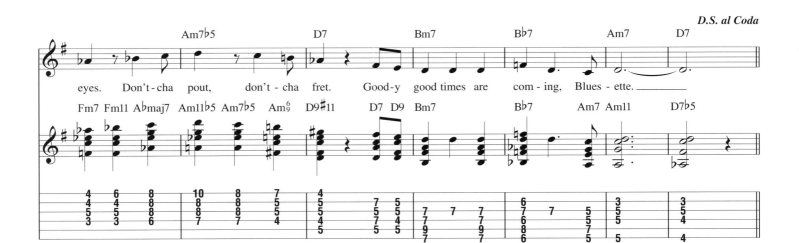

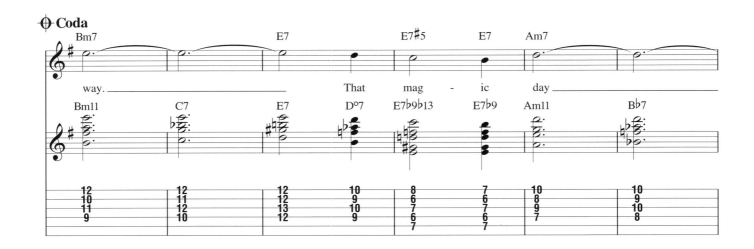

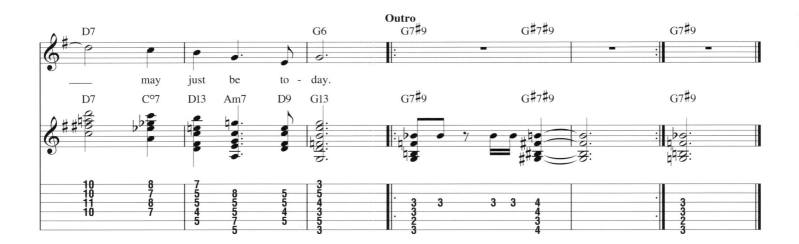

Additional Lyrics

2. Long as there's love in our heart to share,
   Dear Bluesette, don't despair.
   Some blue boy is longing just like you,
   To find a someone to be true to.
   Two loving arms he can nestle in and stay.

The Folks Who Live on the Hill

Lyrics by Oscar Hammerstein II
Music by Jerome Kern

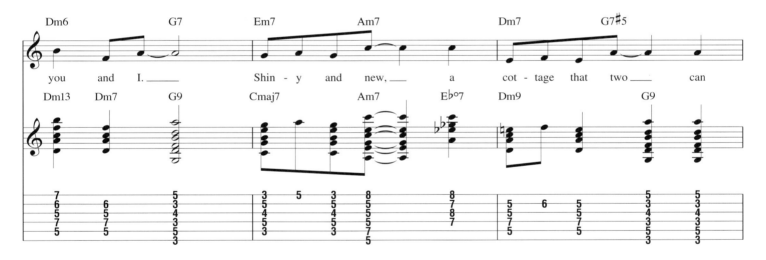

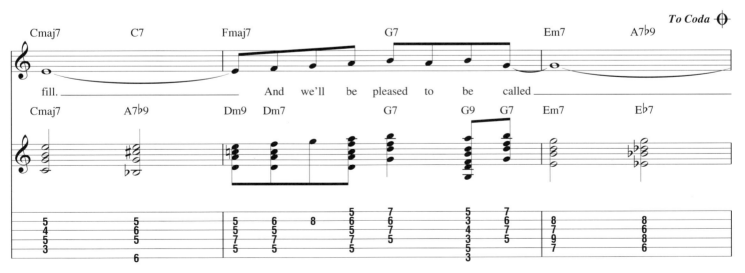

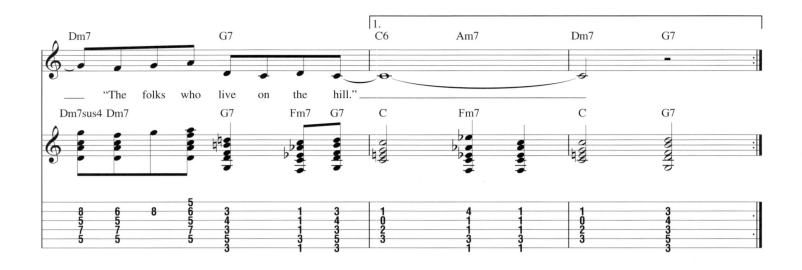

"The folks who live on the hill."

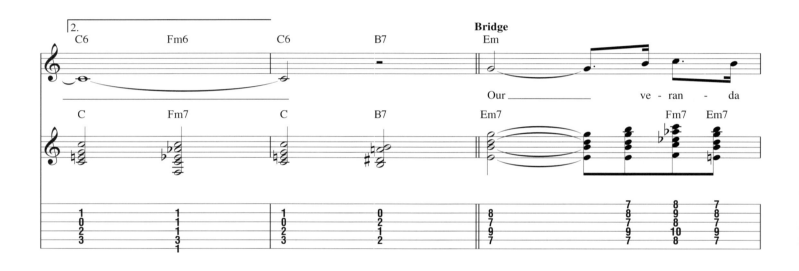

Our _____ ve - ran - da

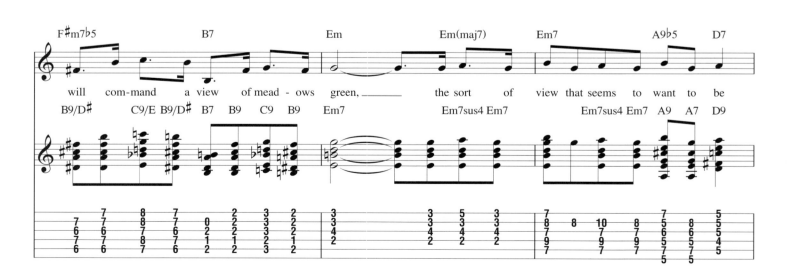

will com-mand a view of mead - ows green, _____ the sort of view that seems to want to be

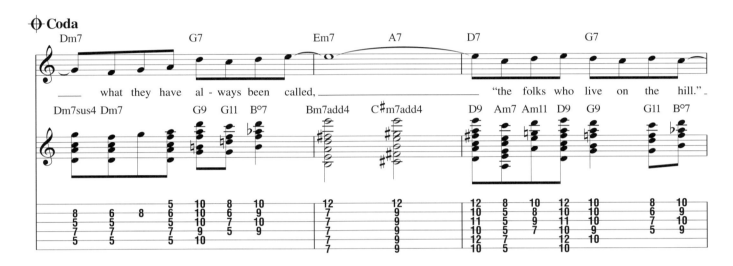

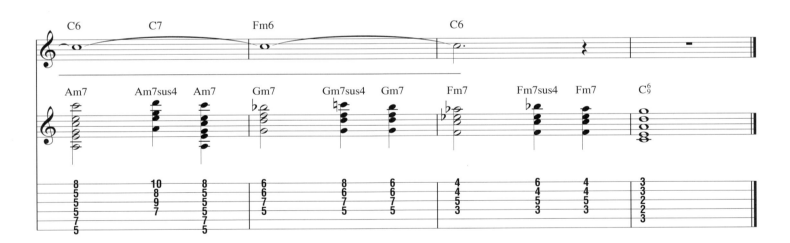

Additional Lyrics

2. Someday we may be adding a thing or two, a wing or two,
   We will make changes as any fam'ly will.
   But we will always be called,
   "The folks who live on the hill."

3. And when the kids grow up and leave us,
   We'll sit and look at that same old view, just we two.
   Darby and Joan, who used to be Jack and Jill,
   The folks who like to be called
   What they have always been called,
   "The folks who live on the hill."

Broadway

Words and Music by Bill Byrd, Teddy McRae and Henri Woode

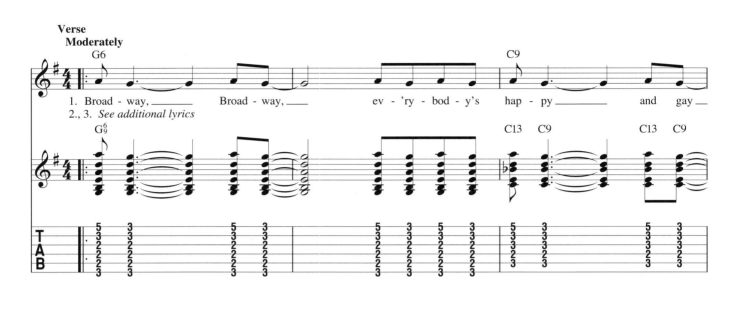

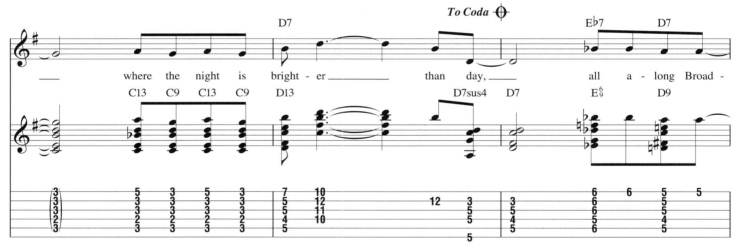

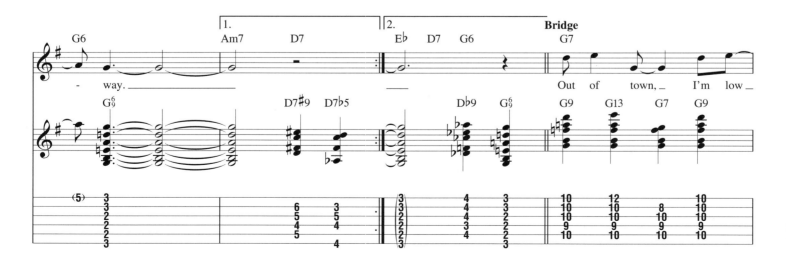

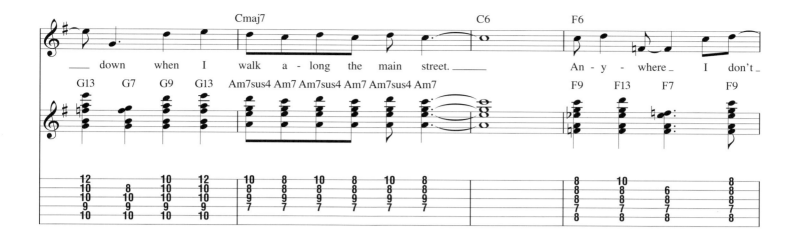

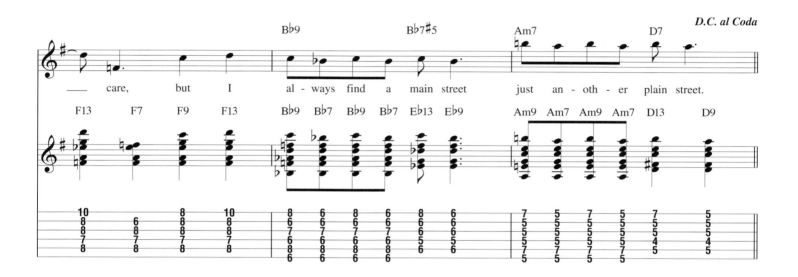

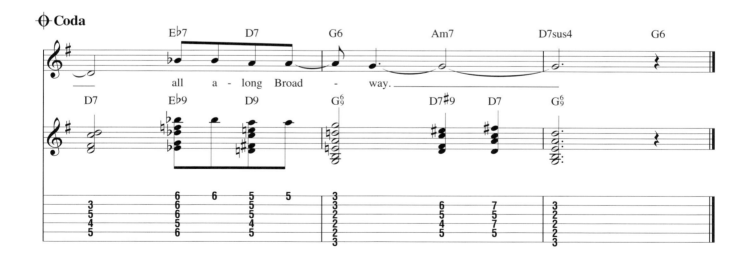

Additional Lyrics

2. Sweethearts and beaus, on their way to movies and shows,
   Dressed up in their Sunday best clothes up and down Broadway.

3. Broadway, Broadway, take a little time out for play
   Where the joy of living holds sway, all along Broadway.

Can't Help Lovin' Dat Man

Lyrics by Oscar Hammerstein II
Music by Jerome Kern

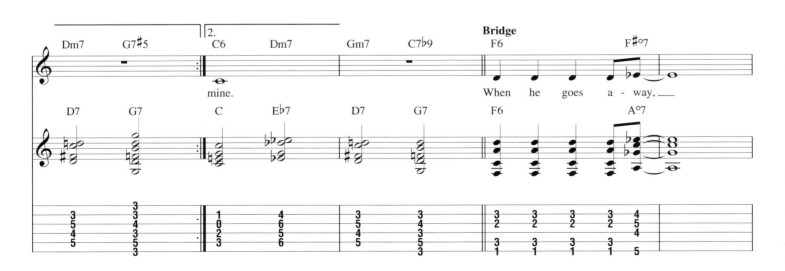

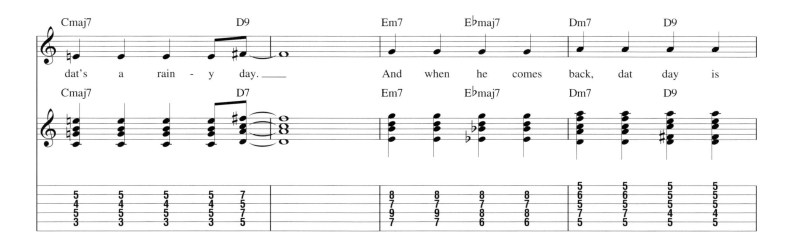

dat's a rain-y day. ____ And when he comes back, dat day is

D.C. al Coda

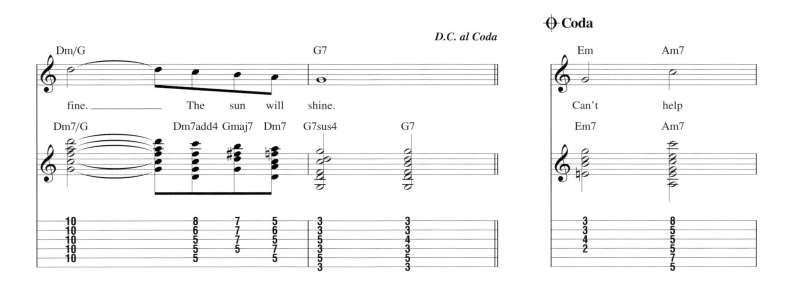

Coda

fine. ____ The sun will shine.

Can't help

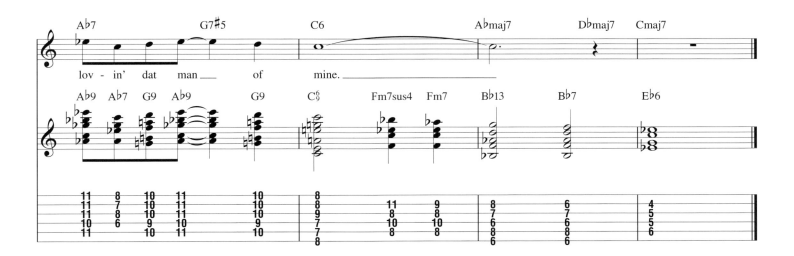

lov - in' dat man ____ of mine. ____

Additional Lyrics

2. Tell me he's lazy, tell me he's slow.
   Tell me I'm crazy, maybe I know.
   Can't help lovin' dat man of mine.

3. He can come home as late as can be.
   Home without him ain't no home to me.
   Can't help lovin' dat man of mine.

Dearly Beloved

Music by Jerome Kern
Words by Johnny Mercer

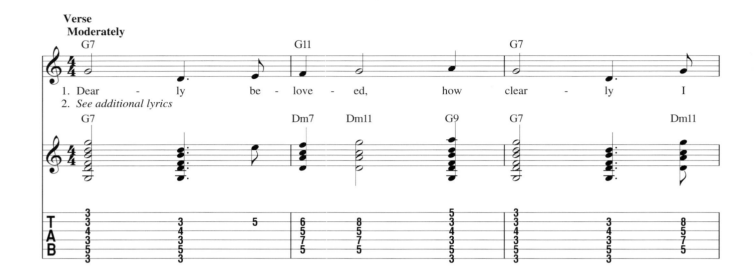

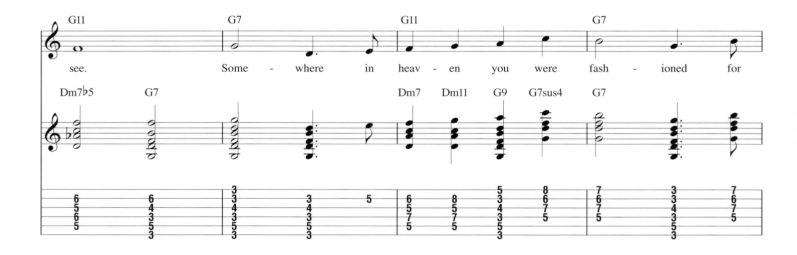

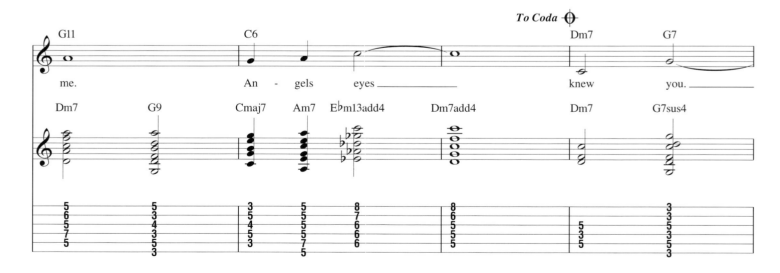

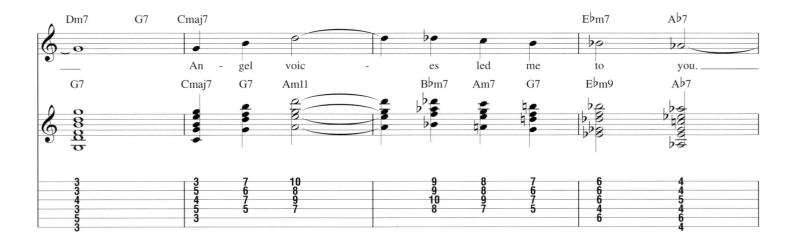

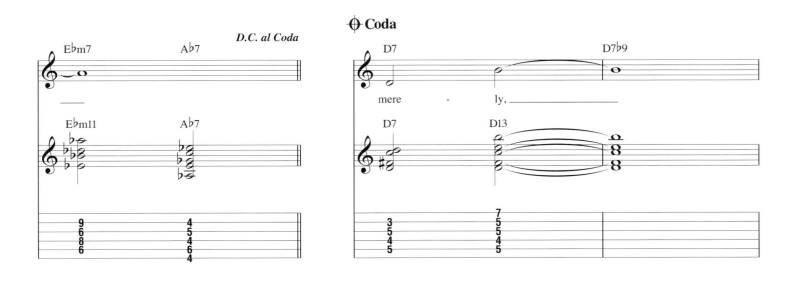

⊕ Coda

D.C. al Coda

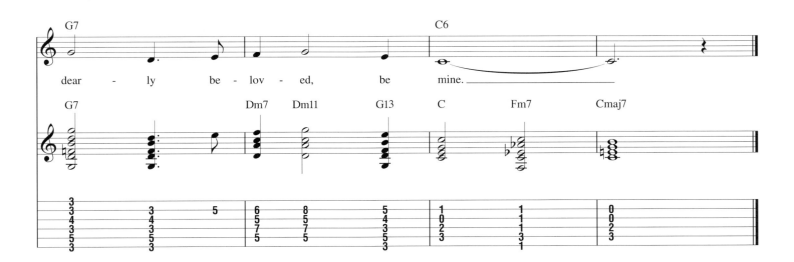

Additional Lyrics

2. Nothing can stop me. Fate gave me a sign.
   I know that I'll be yours come shower or shine.
   So, I say merely, dearly beloved be mine.

Dreamsville

Lyrics by Jay Livingston and Ray Evans
Music by Henry Mancini

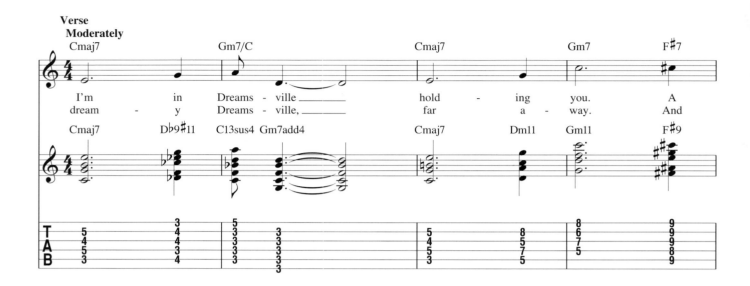

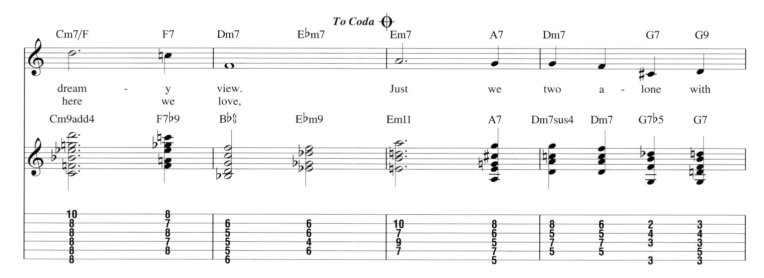

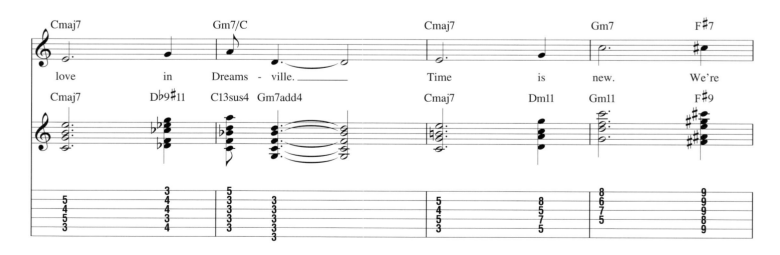

A Fine Romance

Words by Dorothy Fields
Music by Jerome Kern

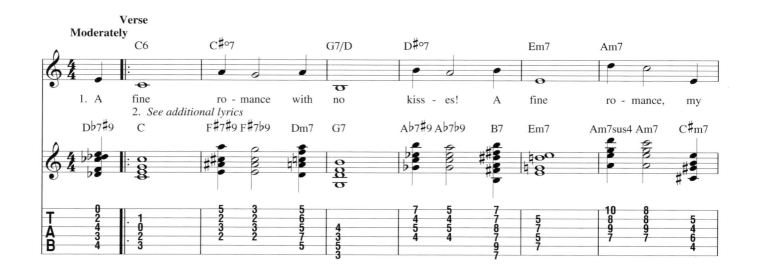

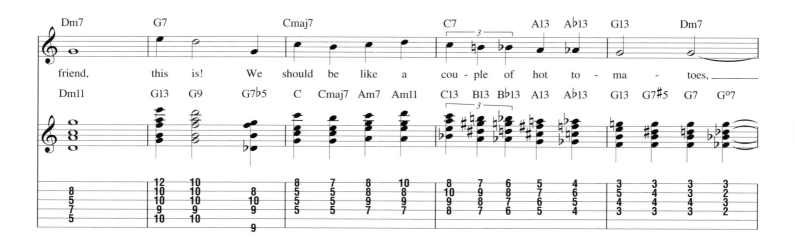

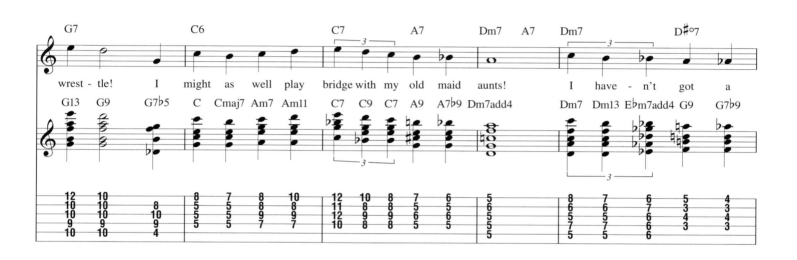

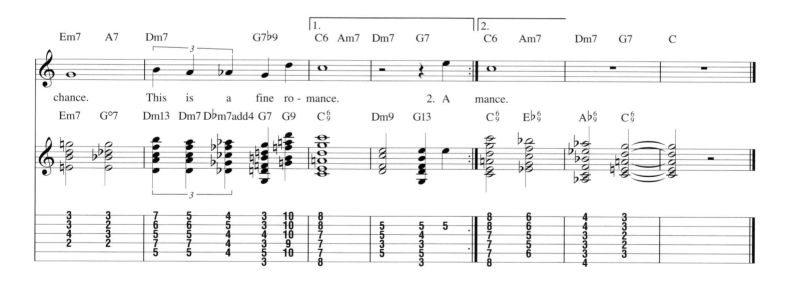

Additional Lyrics

2. A fine romance my good fellow!
   You take romance, I'll take jello!
   You're calmer than the seal in the Arctic Ocean,
   At least they flap their fins to express emotion.
   A fine romance with no quarrels,
   With no insults, and all morals!
   I've never mussed the crease in your blue serge pants!
   I never get the chance. This is a fine romance.

For Heaven's Sake

Words and Music by Don Meyer, Elise Bretton and Sherman Edwards

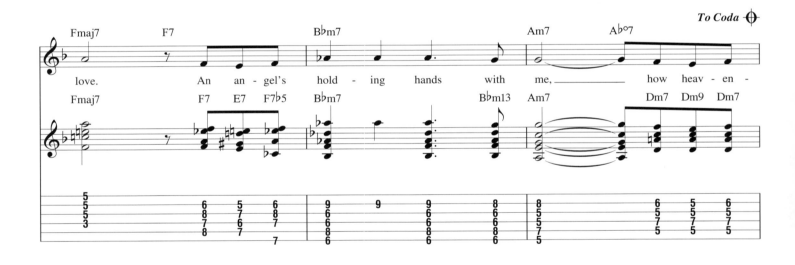

Bridge

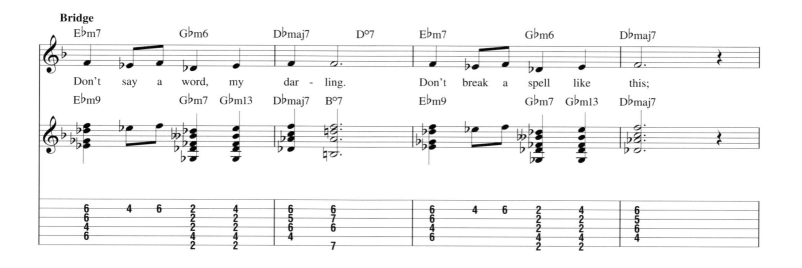

Don't say a word, my dar - ling. Don't break a spell like this;

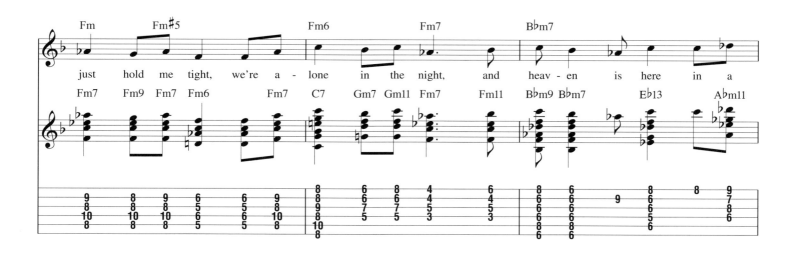

just hold me tight, we're a - lone in the night, and heav - en is here in a

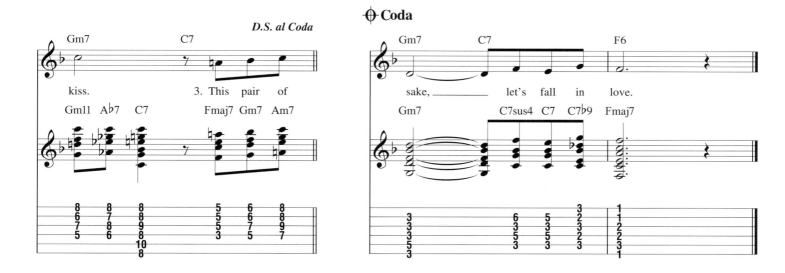

D.S. al Coda

kiss. 3. This pair of

Coda

sake, _____ let's fall in love.

Additional Lyrics

2. Here is romance for us to try.
   Here is the chance we can't deny.
   While heaven's giving us the break,
   Let's fall in love, for heaven's sake.

3. This pair of eyes can see a star;
   So paradise can't be so far.
   Since heaven's what we're dreaming of,
   For heaven's sake, let's fall in love.

The Girl from Ipanema
(Garôta de Ipanema)

Music by Antonio Carlos Jobim
English Words by Norman Gimbel
Original Words by Vinicius de Moraes

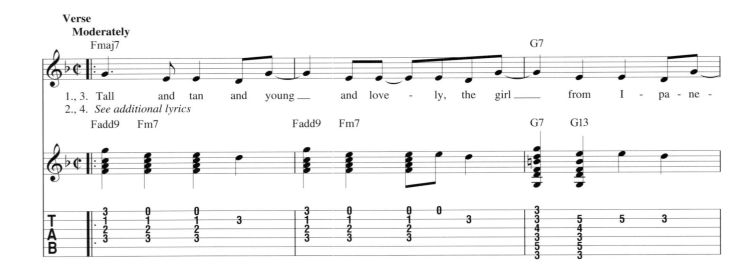

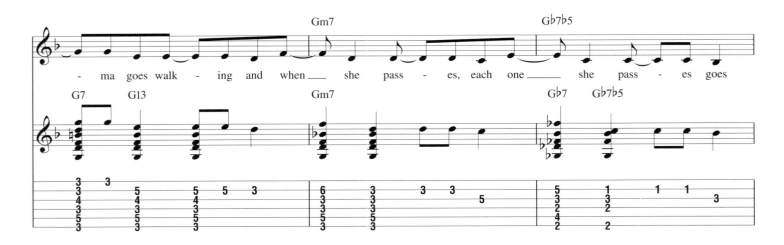

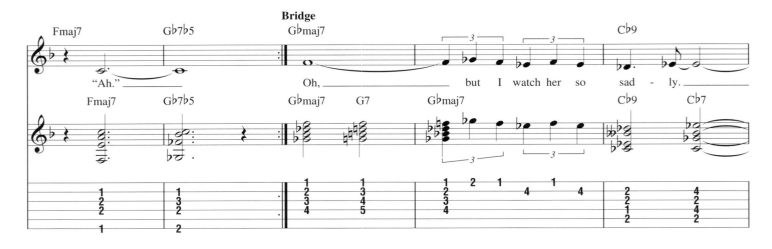

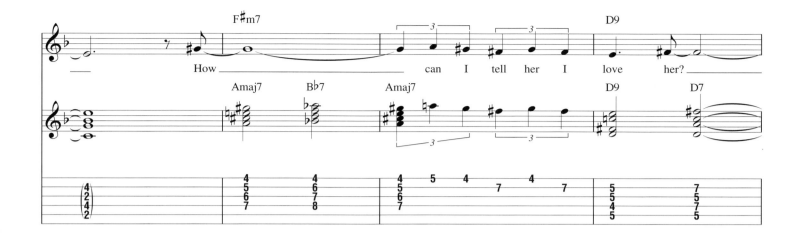

How _____ can I tell her I love her? _____

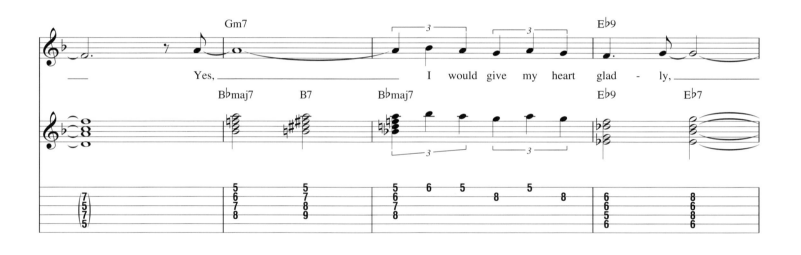

Yes, _____ I would give my heart glad - ly, _____

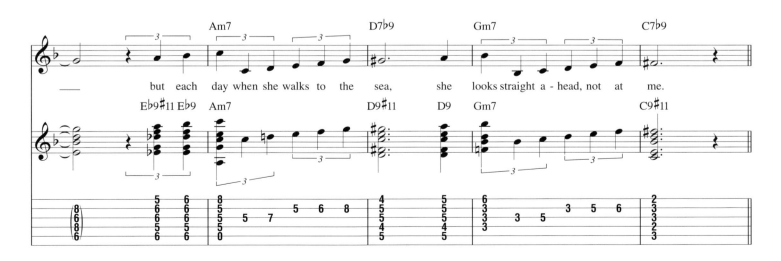

_____ but each day when she walks to the sea, she looks straight a - head, not at me.

Outro-Verse

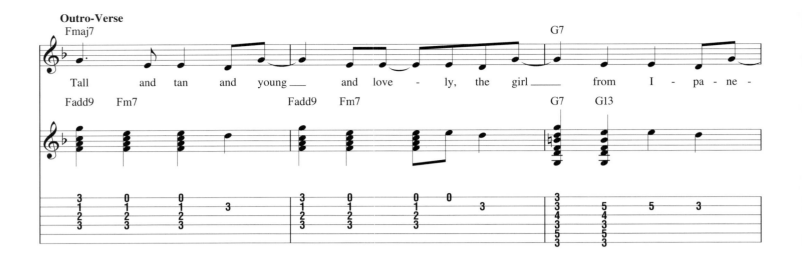

Tall and tan and young ___ and love - ly, the girl ___ from I - pa - ne -

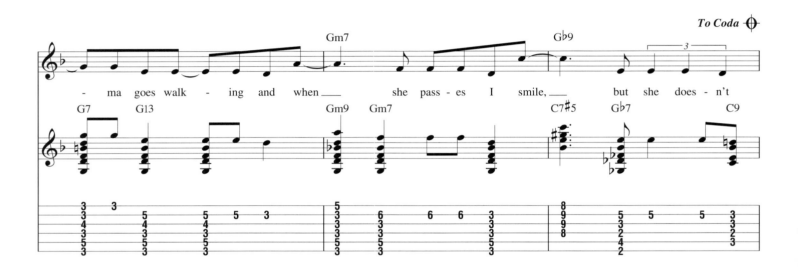

- ma goes walk - ing and when ___ she pass - es I smile, ___ but she does - n't

To Coda ⊕

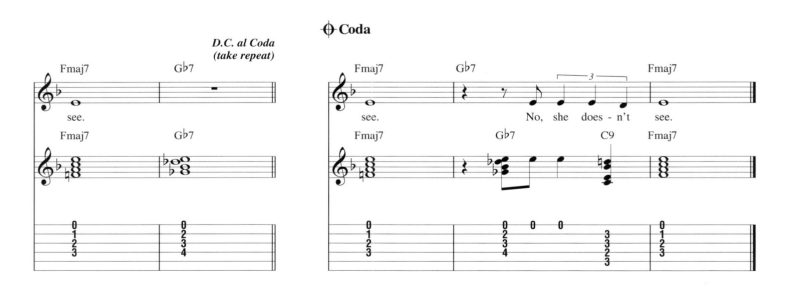

⊕ **Coda**

D.C. al Coda (take repeat)

see.

see.

No, she does - n't see.

Additional Lyrics

2., 4. When she walks, she's like a samba that
Swings so cool and sways so gentle, that
When she passes, each one she passes goes, "Ah."

I'll Never Smile Again

Words and Music by Ruth Lowe

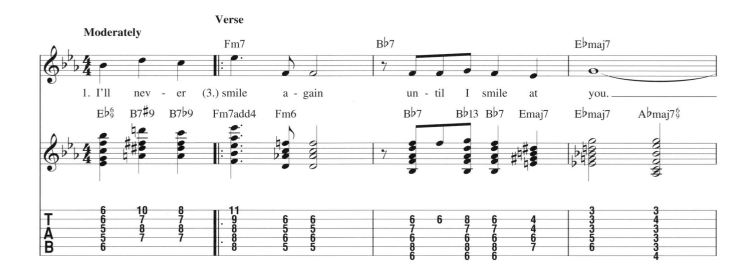

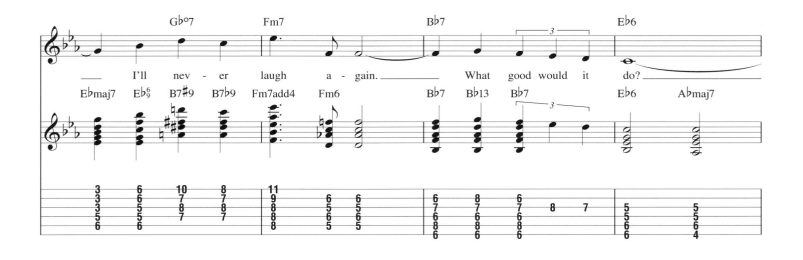

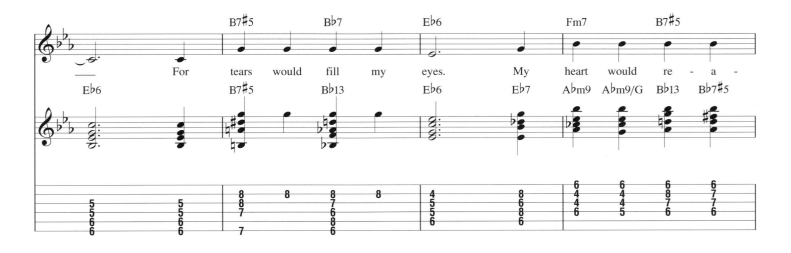

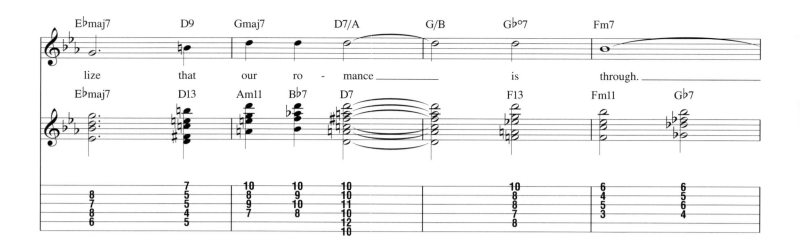

lize that our ro - mance _____ is through. _____

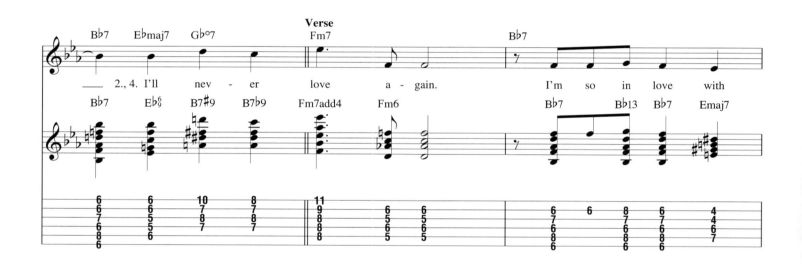

2., 4. I'll nev - er love a - gain. I'm so in love with

you. _____ I'll nev - er thrill a - gain _____ to some - bod - y

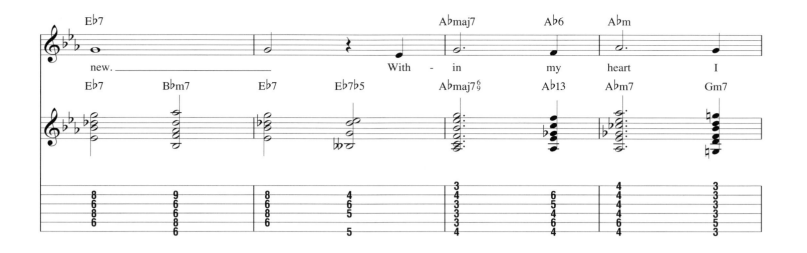

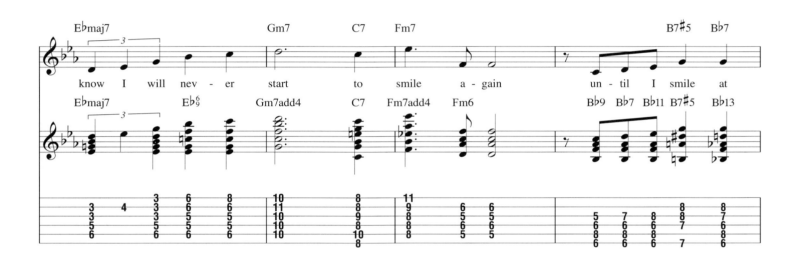

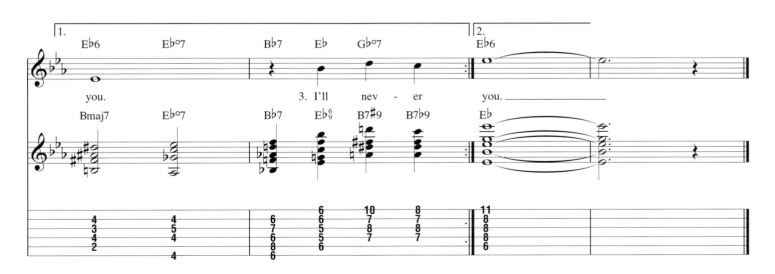

How High the Moon

Words by Nancy Hamilton
Music by Morgan Lewis

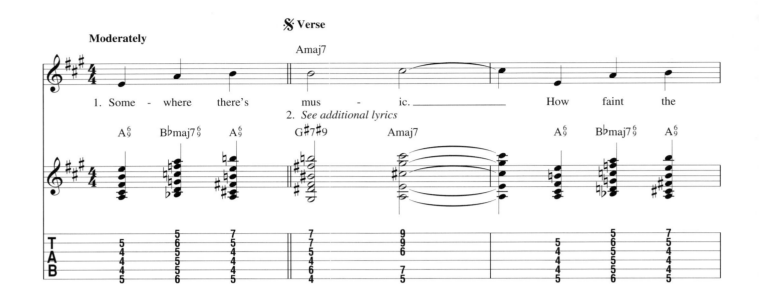

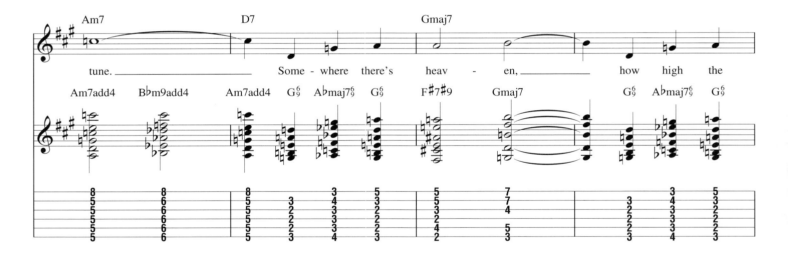

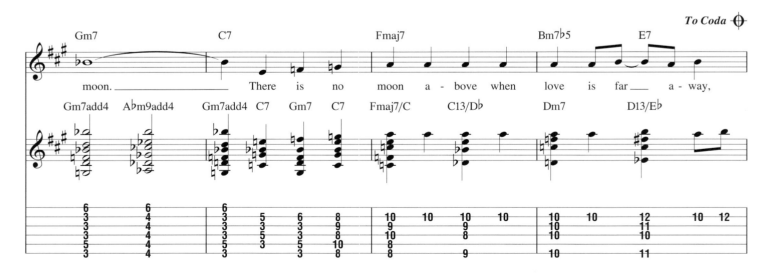

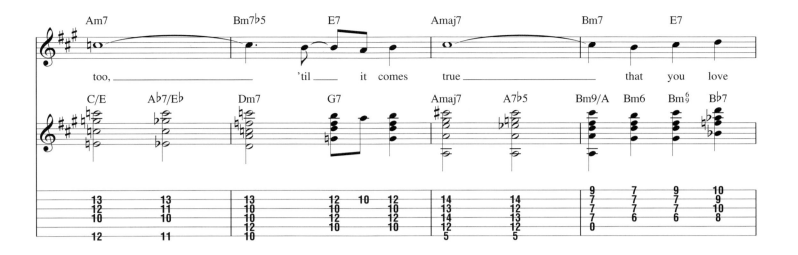

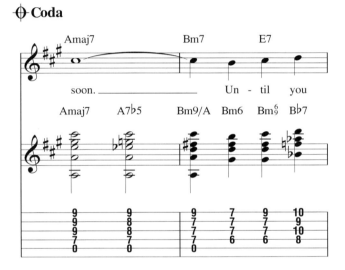

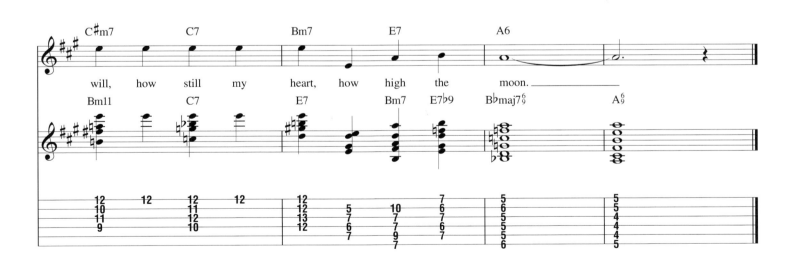

Additional Lyrics

2. Somewhere there's music. It's where you are.
   Somewhere there's heaven, how near, how far.
   The darkest night would shine if you would come to me soon.
   Until you will, how still my heart, how high the moon.

I Love Paris

Words and Music by Cole Porter

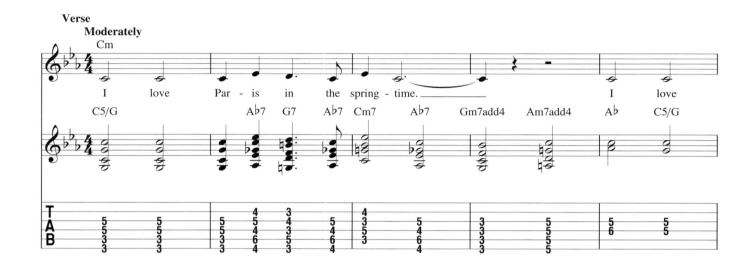

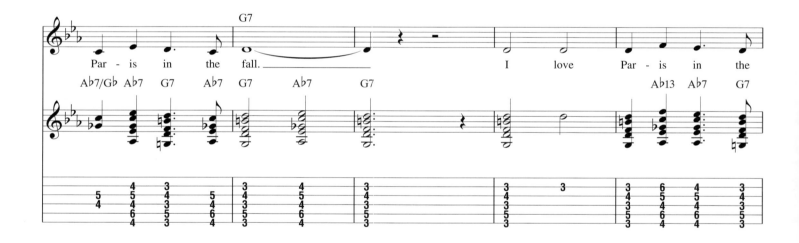

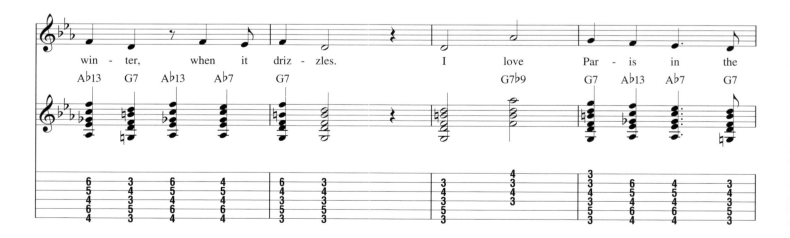

I'm Beginning to See the Light

Words and Music by Don George, Johnny Hodges, Duke Ellington and Harry James

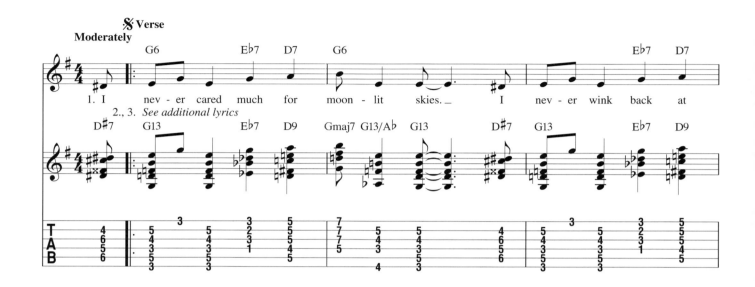

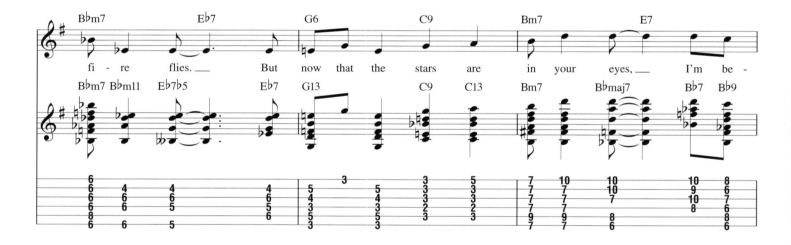

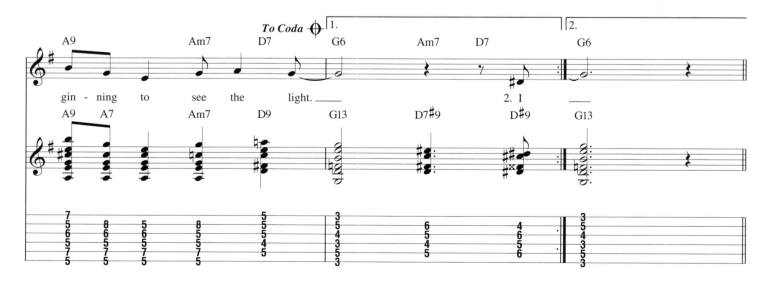

Bridge

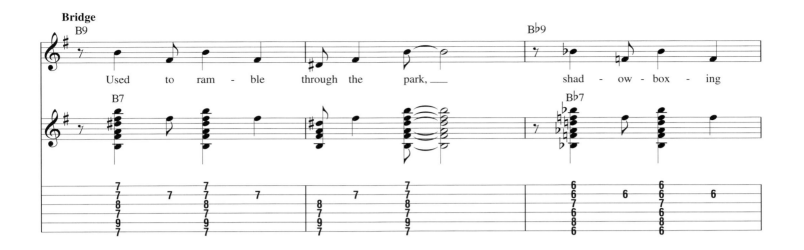

Used to ram-ble through the park, ____ shad-ow-box-ing

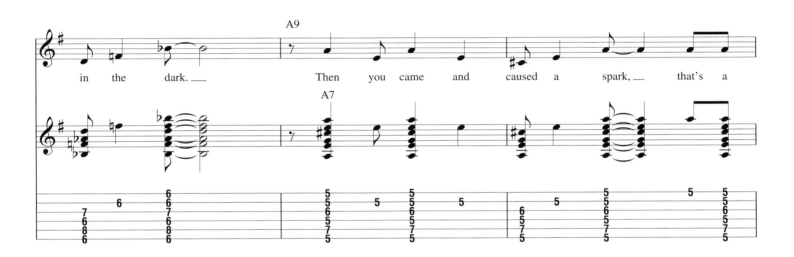

in the dark. ____ Then you came and caused a spark, ____ that's a

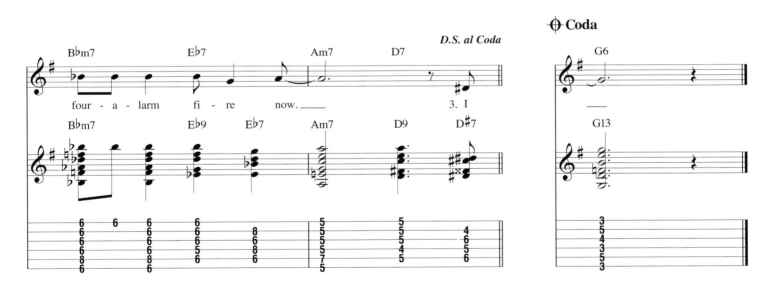

four-a-larm fi-re now. ____

D.S. al Coda

3. I

Coda

Additional Lyrics

2. I never went in for afterglow,
   Or candlelight on the mistletoe.
   But now when you turn the lamp down low,
   I'm beginning to see the light.

3. I never made love by lantern shine.
   I never saw rainbows in my wine.
   But now that your lips are burning mine,
   I'm beginning to see the light.

I'm Just a Lucky So and So

Words by Mack David
Music by Duke Ellington

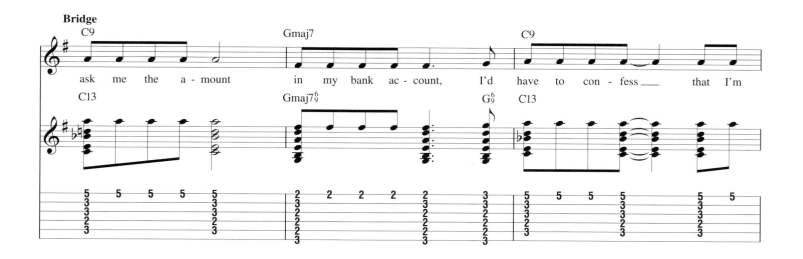

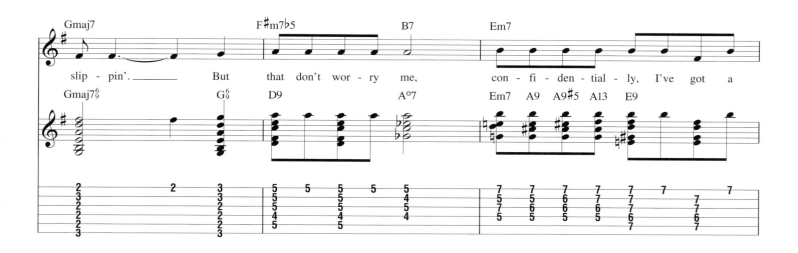

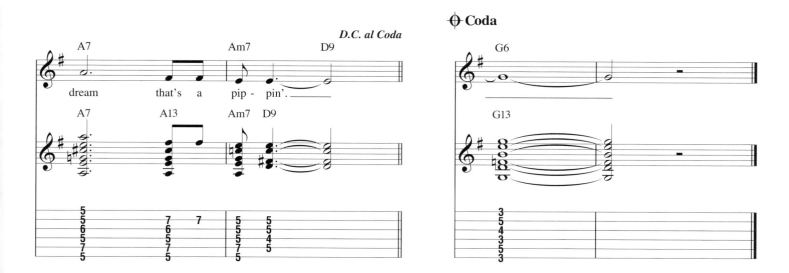

Additional Lyrics

2. The birds in ev'ry tree are all so neighborly.
   They sing wherever I go.
   I guess I'm just a luck so and so.

3. And when the day is through, each night I hurry to
   A home where love waits, I know.
   I guess I'm just a lucky so and so.

I'm Old Fashioned

from YOU WERE NEVER LOVELIER

Words by Johnny Mercer
Music by Jerome Kern

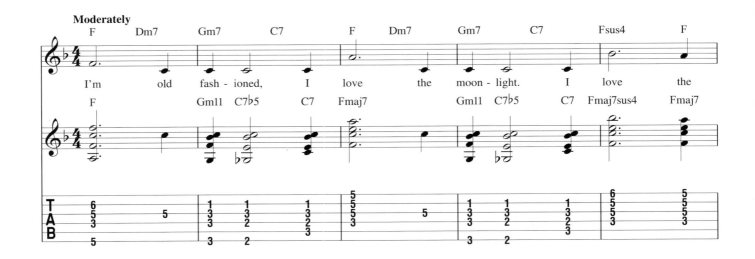

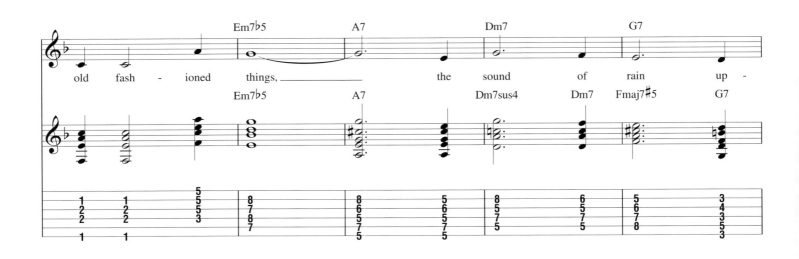

It's Easy to Remember

from the Paramount Picture MISSISSIPPI

Words by Lorenz Hart
Music by Richard Rodgers

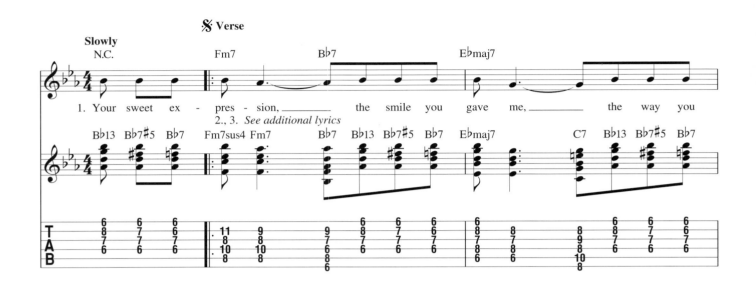

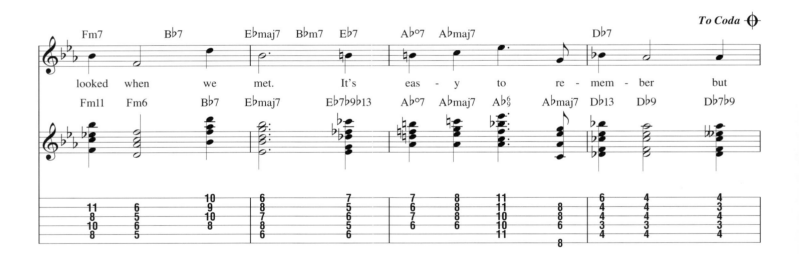

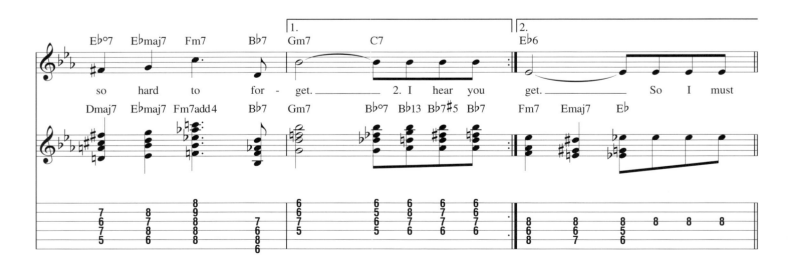

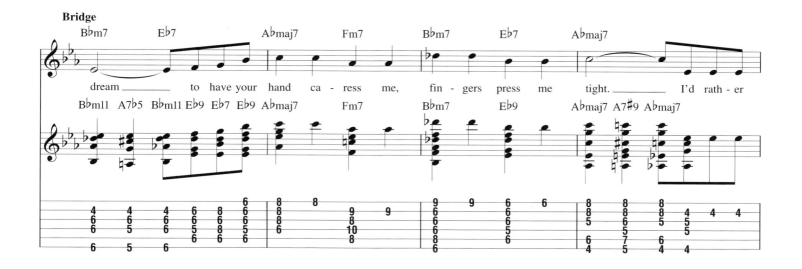

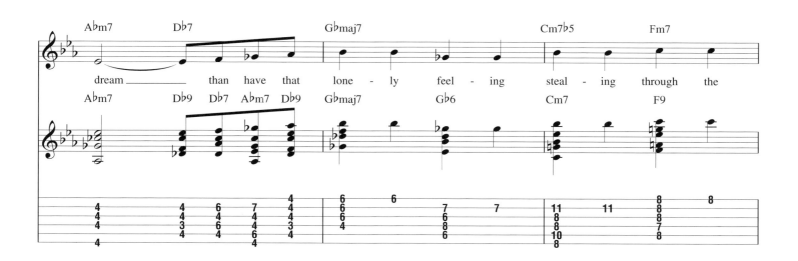

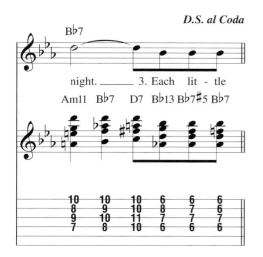

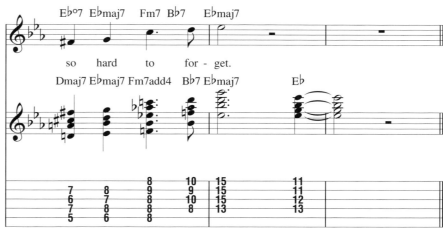

Additional Lyrics

2. I hear you whisper, "I'll always love you!"
   I know it's over, and yet,
   It's easy to remember, but so hard to forget.

3. Each little moment is clear before me,
   And though it brings me regret,
   It's easy to remember, and so hard to forget.

Long Ago (And Far Away)

Words by Ira Gershwin
Music by Jerome Kern

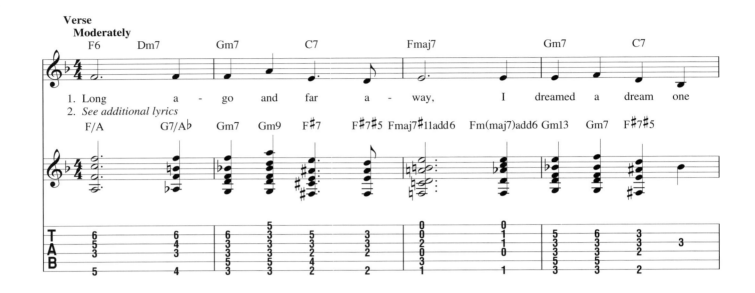

1. Long a - go and far a - way, I dreamed a dream one
2. *See additional lyrics*

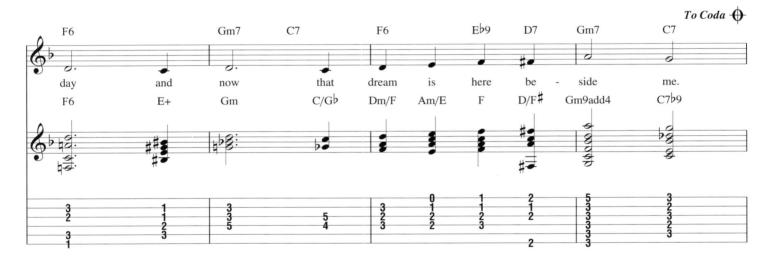

day and now that dream is here be - side me.

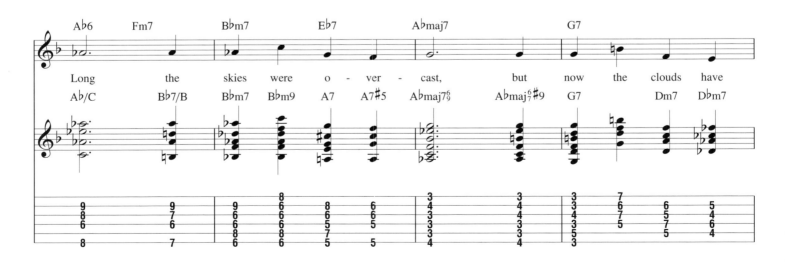

Long the skies were o - ver - cast, but now the clouds have

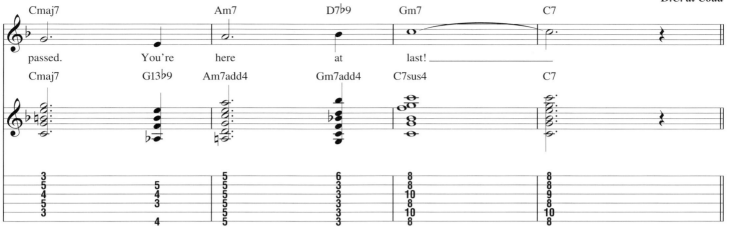

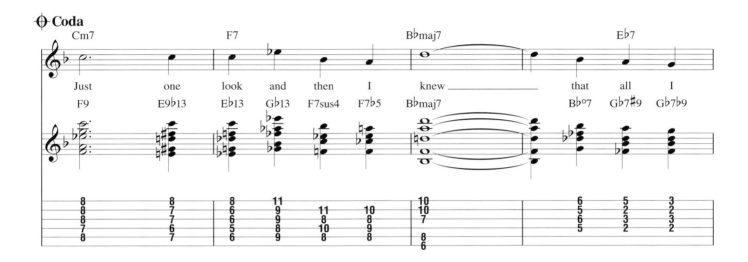

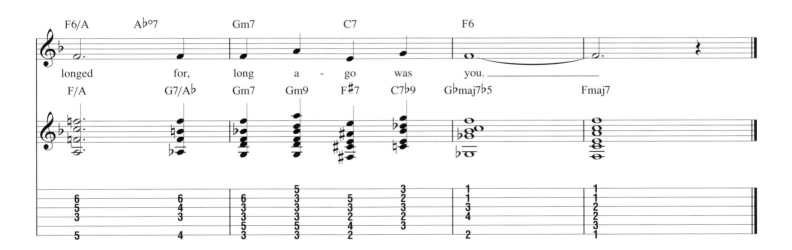

Additional Lyrics

2. Chills run up and down my spine. Aladdin's lamp is mine.
   The dream I dreamed was not denied me.
   Just one look and then I knew
   That all I longed for, long ago was you.

Lover Man (Oh, Where Can You Be?)

By Jimmy Davis, Roger Ramirez and Jimmy Sherman

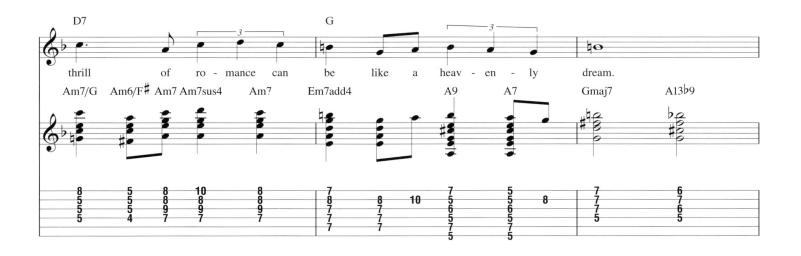

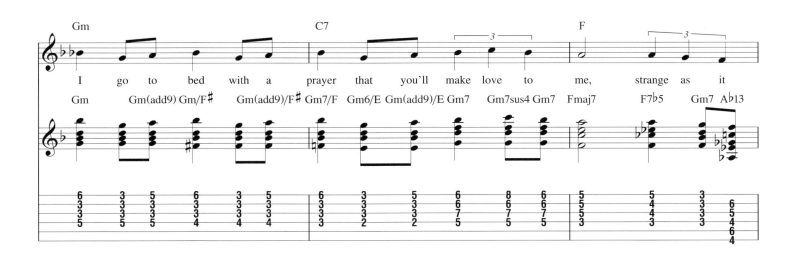

Additional Lyrics

2. The night is cold, and I'm so all alone,
   I'd give my soul just to call you my own.
   Got a moon above me, but no one to love me.
   Lover man, oh where can you be?

3. Some day we'll meet and you'll dry all my tears,
   Then whisper sweet little things in my ears.
   Huggin' and kissin', oh, what I've been missin'.
   Lover man, oh where can you be?

A Man and a Woman
(Un Homme et une Femme)

from A MAN AND A WOMAN

Original Words by Pierre Barouh
English Words by Jerry Keller
Music by Francis Lai

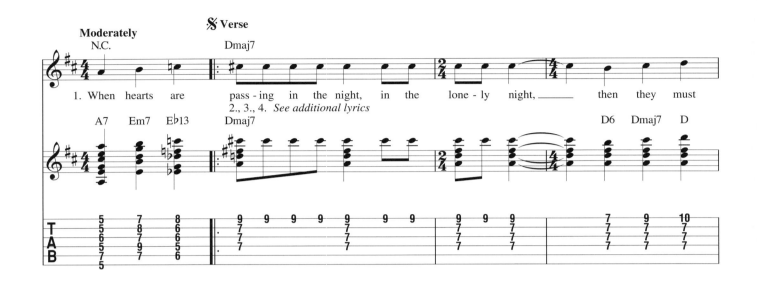

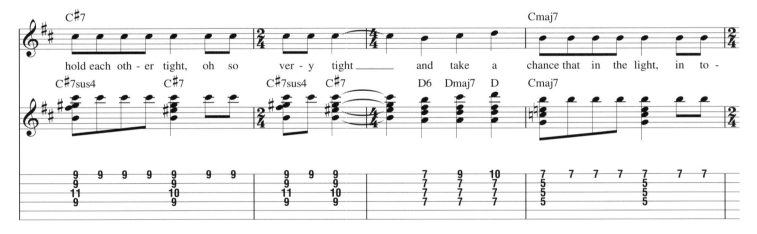

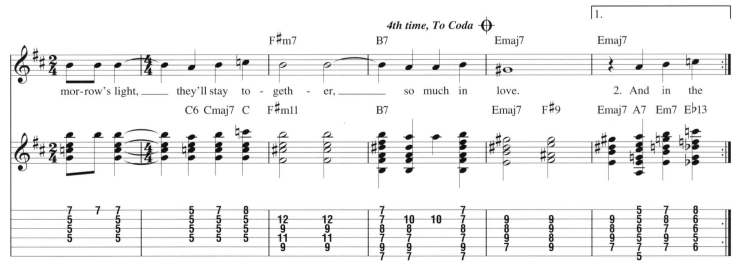

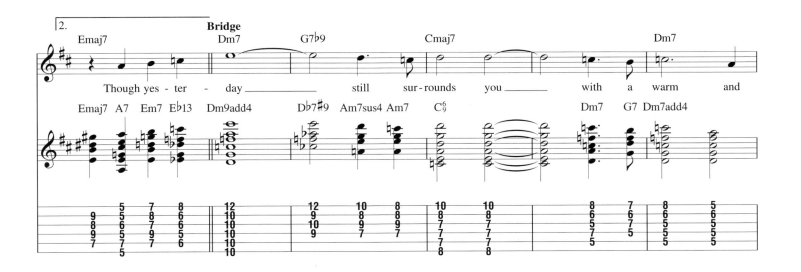

Though yes - ter - day _____ still sur - rounds you _____ with a warm and

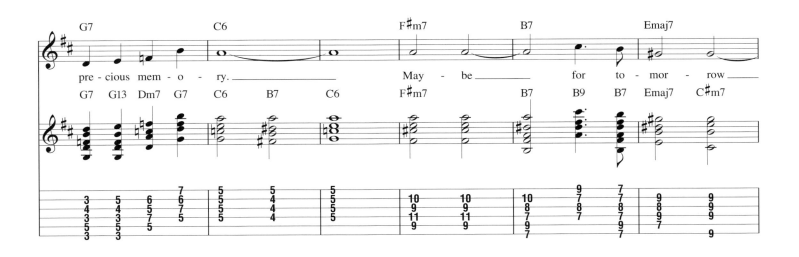

pre - cious mem - o - ry. _____ May - be _____ for to - mor - row

D.S. al Coda
(take repeat)

_____ we can build a new dream _____ for you and me. 3. This glow we

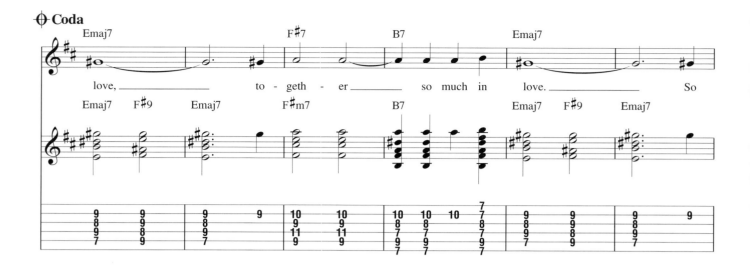

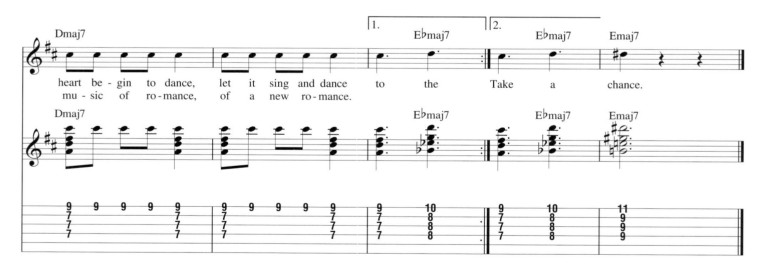

Additional Lyrics

2. And in the silence of the mist, of the morning mist,
   When lips are waiting to be kissed, longing to be kissed,
   Where is the reason to resist and deny a kiss
   That holds a promise of happiness?

3. This glow we feel is something rare, something really rare.
   So come and say you want to share, want to really share
   The beauty waiting for us there, calling for us there,
   That only loving can give the heart.

4. When life is passing in the night, in the rushing night,
   A man, a woman in the night, in the lonely night
   Must take a chance that in the light, in tomorrow's light,
   They'll be together, so much in love,
   Together, so much in love.

Old Devil Moon

Words by E.Y. Harburg
Music by Burton Lane

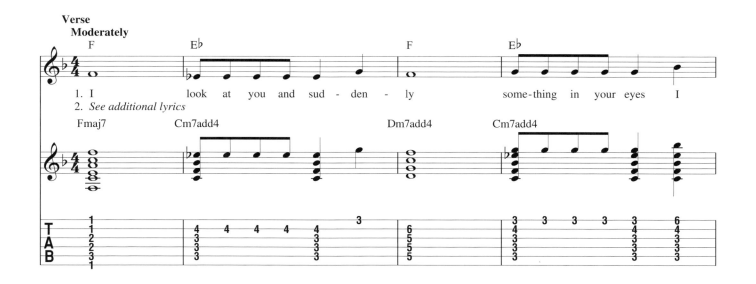

Verse
Moderately

1. I look at you and sud - den - ly some - thing in your eyes I
2. *See additional lyrics*

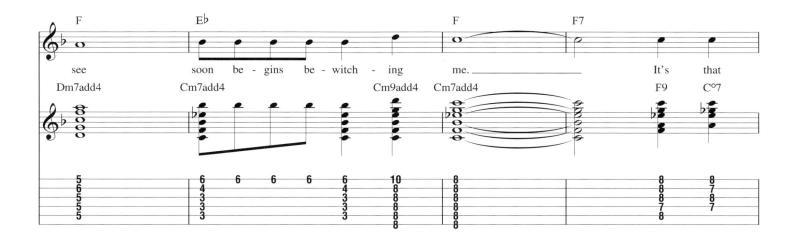

see soon be - gins be - witch - ing me. _____ It's that

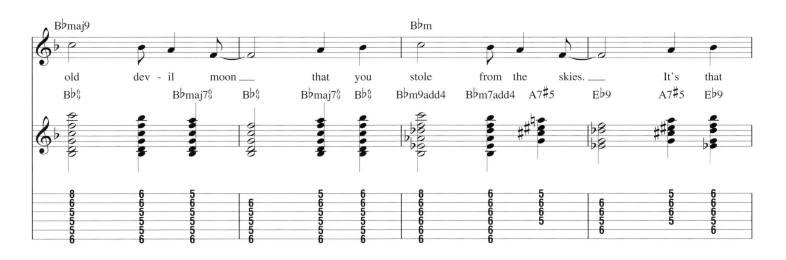

old dev - il moon _____ that you stole from the skies. _____ It's that

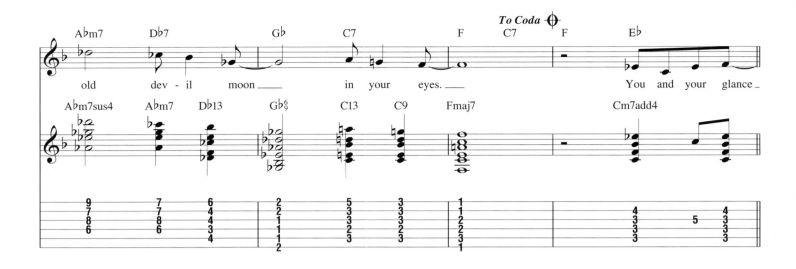

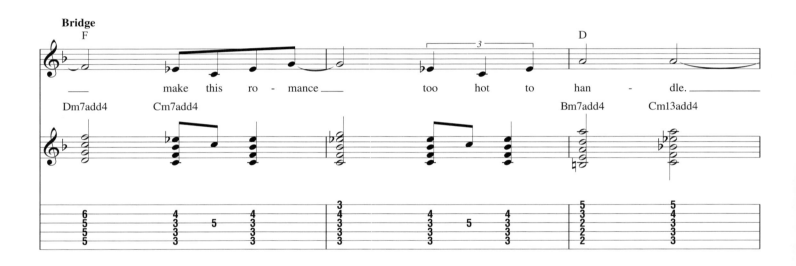

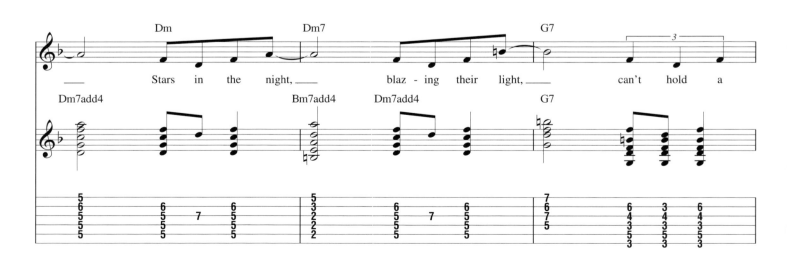

Old Devil Moon

Words by E.Y. Harburg
Music by Burton Lane

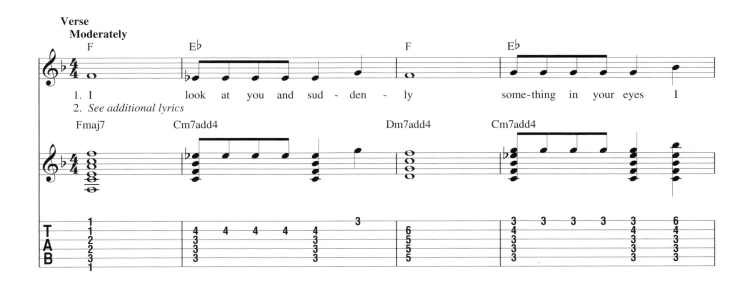

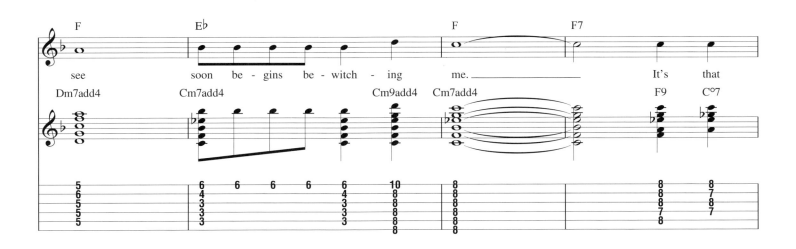

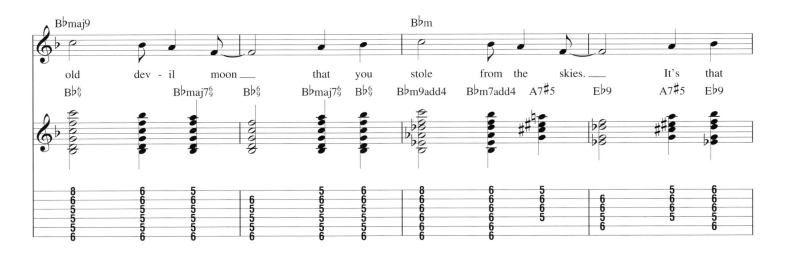

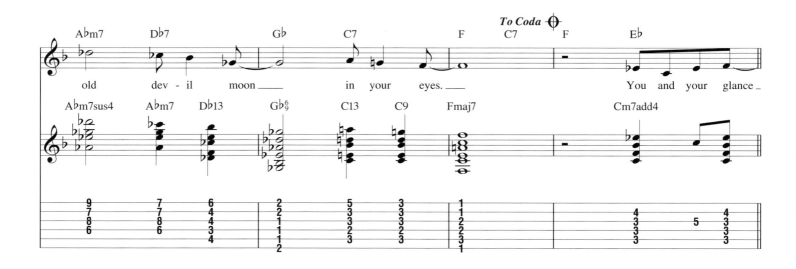

old dev - il moon in your eyes. You and your glance

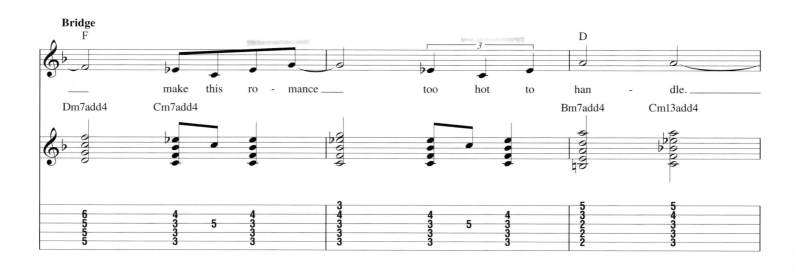

Bridge

make this ro - mance too hot to han - dle.

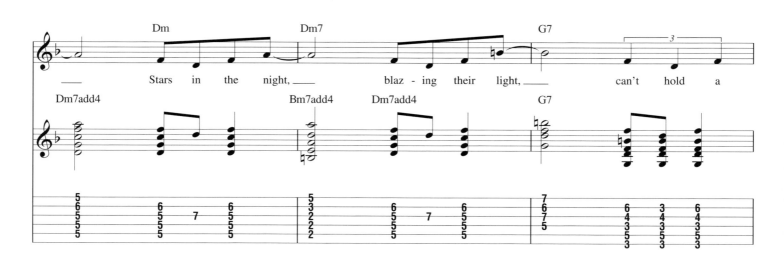

Stars in the night, blaz - ing their light, can't hold a

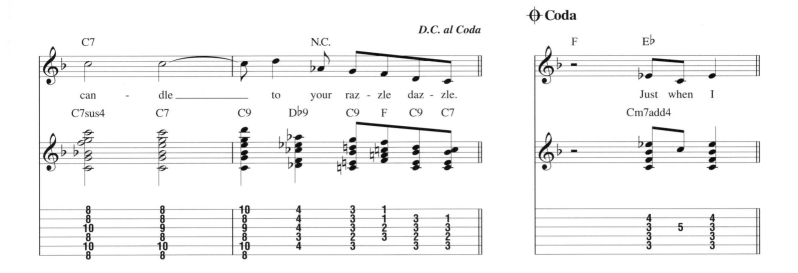

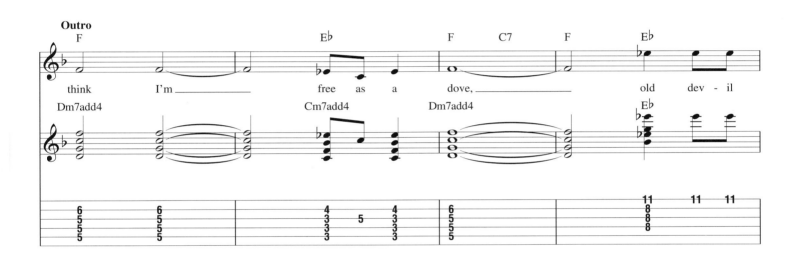

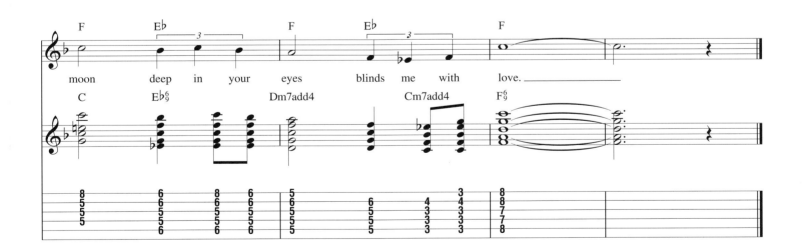

Additional Lyrics

2. You've got me flyin' high and wide
On a magic carpet ride
Full of butterflies inside.
Wanna cry, wanna croon,
Wanna laugh like a loon.
It's that old devil moon in your eyes.

More Than You Know

Words by William Rose and Edward Eliscu
Music by Vincent Youmans

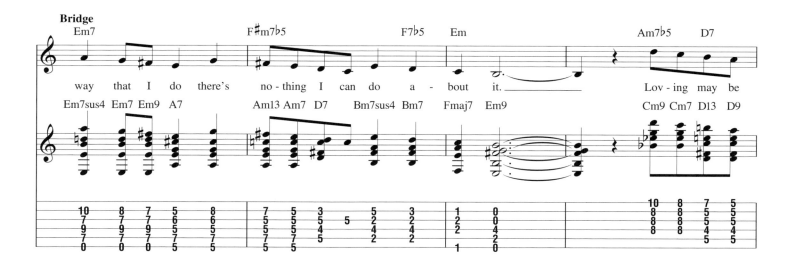

Bridge

way that I do there's no-thing I can do a-bout it. _____ Lov-ing may be

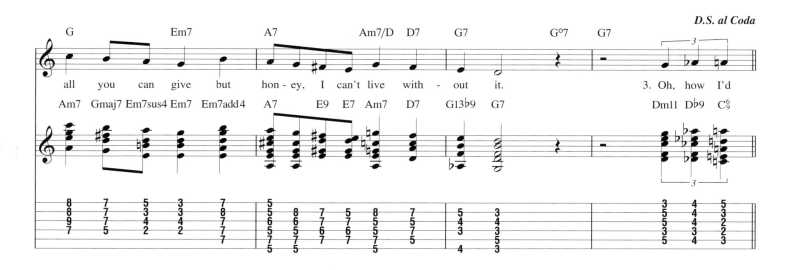

D.S. al Coda

all you can give but hon-ey, I can't live with-out it. 3. Oh, how I'd

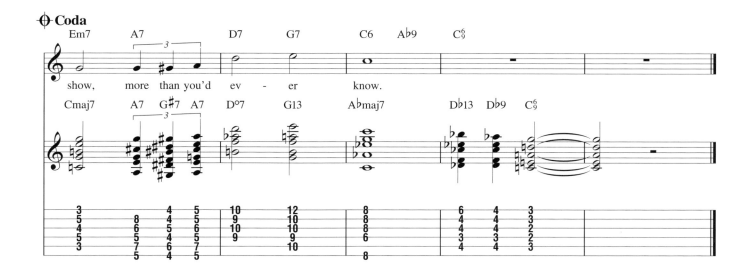

⊕ Coda

show, more than you'd ev-er know.

Additional Lyrics

2. Whether you're right, whether you're wrong,
   Girl of my heart, I'll string along.
   You need me so, more than you'll ever know.

3. Oh, how I'd cry, oh how I'd cry
   If you got tired and said, "good-bye."
   More than I'd show, more than you'd ever know.

Ol' Man River

Lyrics by Oscar Hammerstein II
Music by Jerome Kern

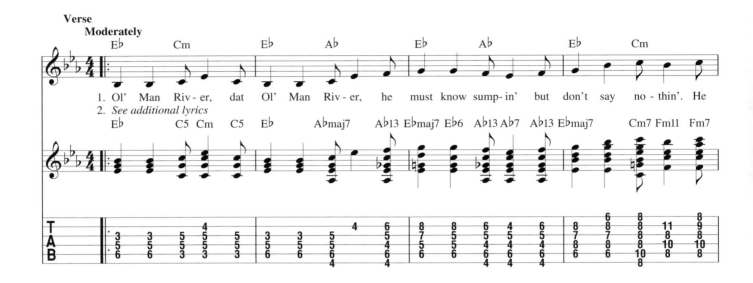

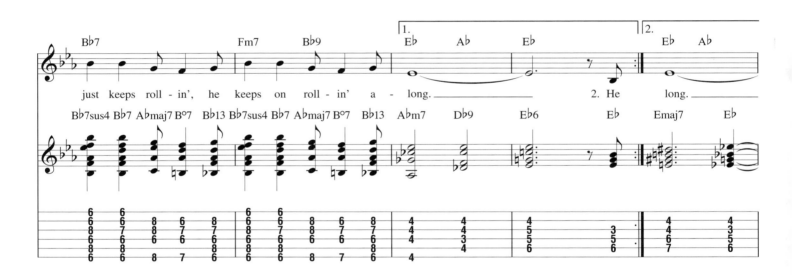

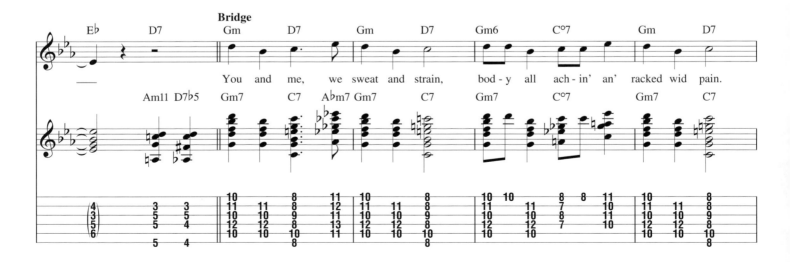

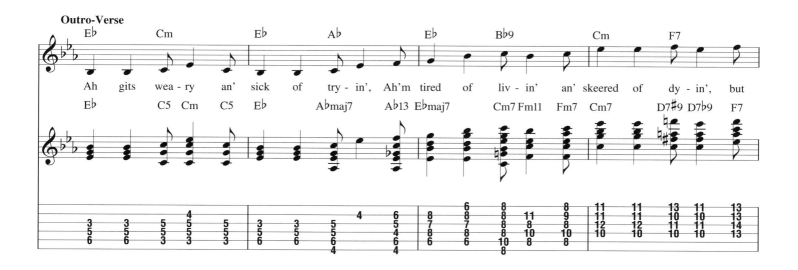

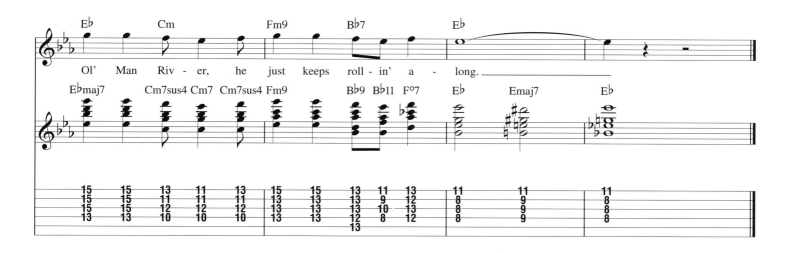

Additional Lyrics

2. He don't plant 'taters, he don't plant cotton,
   An' dem dat plants 'em is soon forgotten.
   But Ol' Man River, he just keeps rollin' along.

One Note Samba
(Samba de Uma Nota So)

Original Lyrics by Newton Mendonca
English Lyrics by Antonio Carlos Jobim
Music by Antonio Carlos Jobim

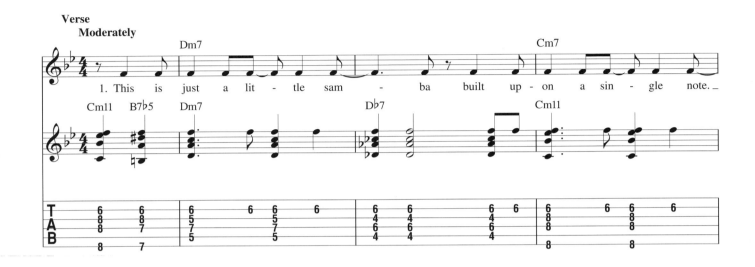

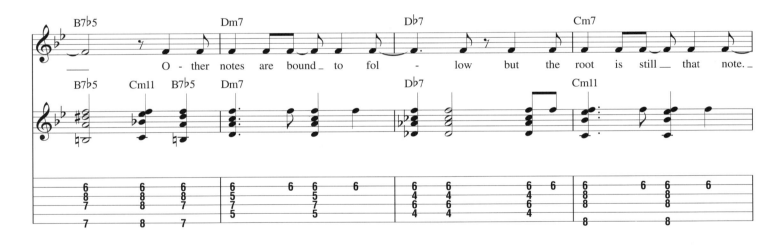

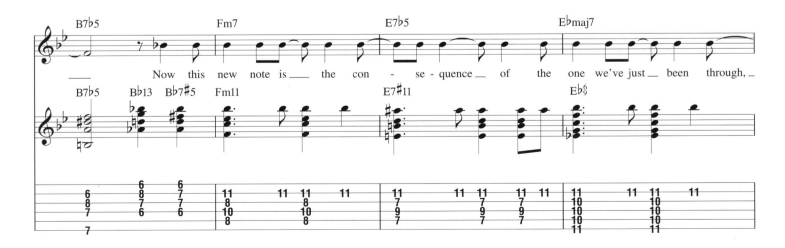

Smoke Gets in Your Eyes

Words by Otto Harbach
Music by Jerome Kern

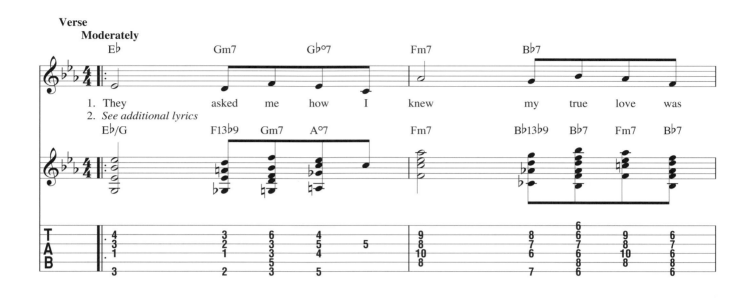

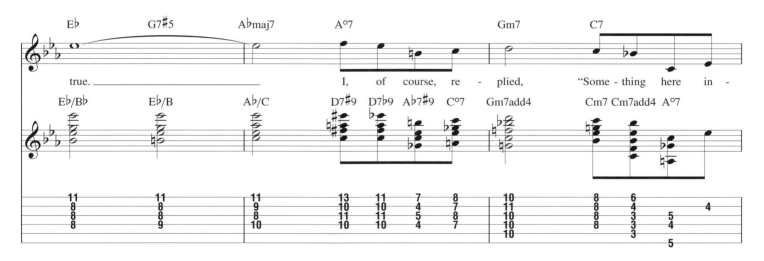

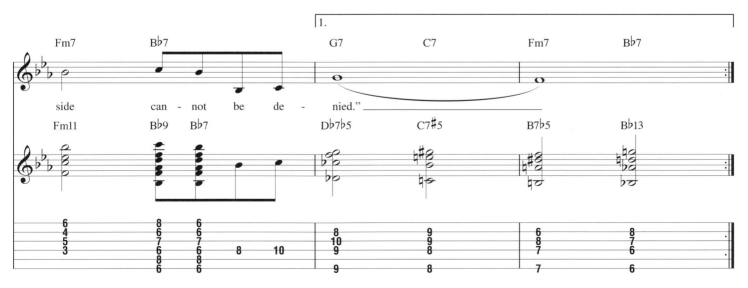

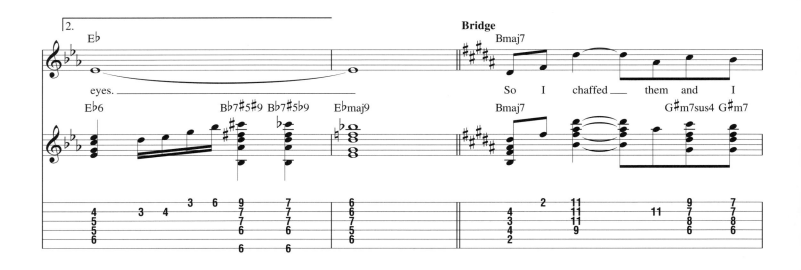

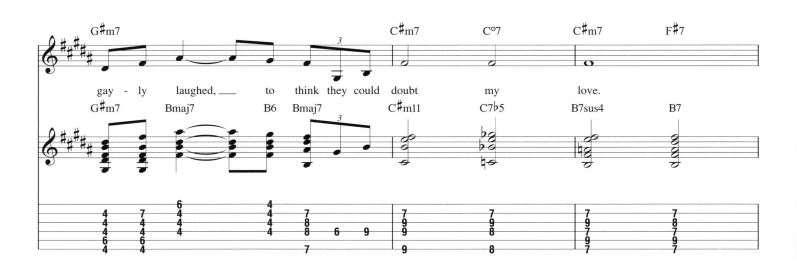

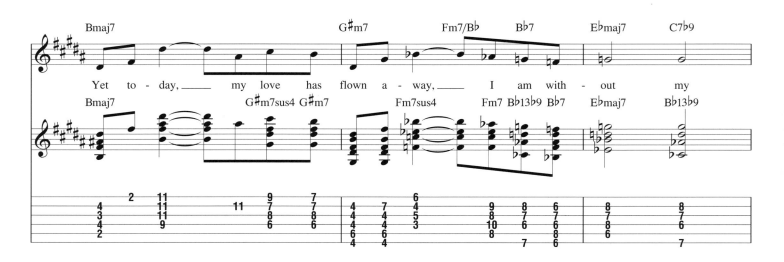

Outro-Verse

love.   Now   laugh - ing   friends   de - ride,   tears   I   can - not

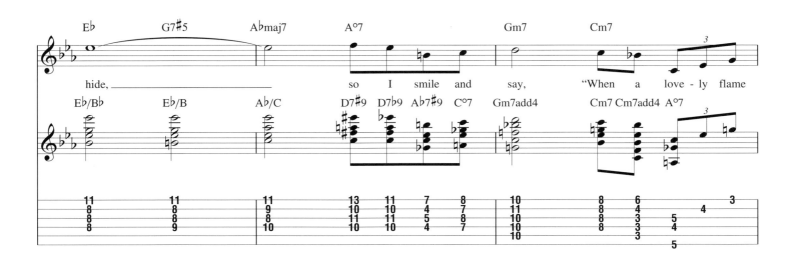

hide, _____   so   I   smile   and   say,   "When   a   love - ly   flame

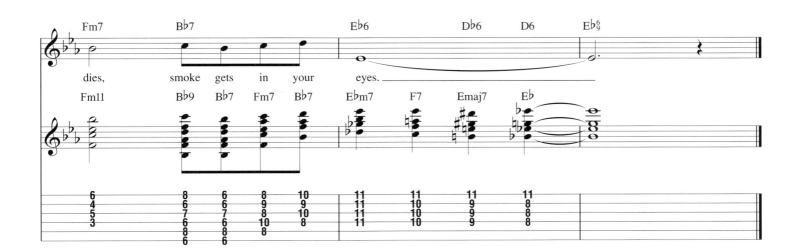

dies,   smoke   gets   in   your   eyes. _____

Additional Lyrics

2. They said some day you'll find
 All who love are blind.
 When your heart's on fire, you must realize
 Smoke gets in your eyes.

The Song Is You

Lyrics by Oscar Hammerstein II
Music by Jerome Kern

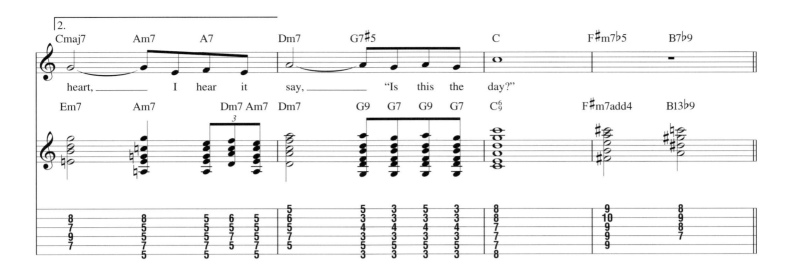

heart, _____ I hear it say, _____ "Is this the day?"

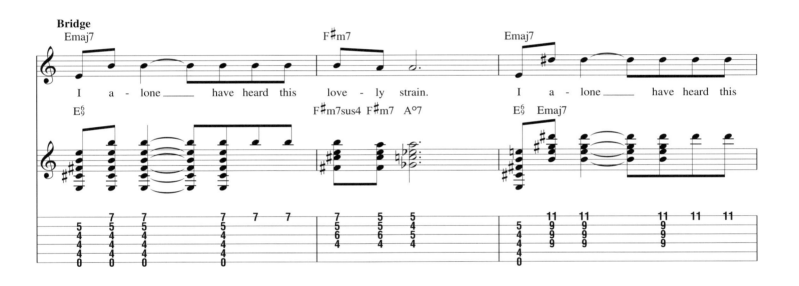

Bridge

I a - lone _____ have heard this love - ly strain. I a - lone _____ have heard this

glad re - frain. Must it be _____ for - ev - er in - side of me? _____ Why can't I

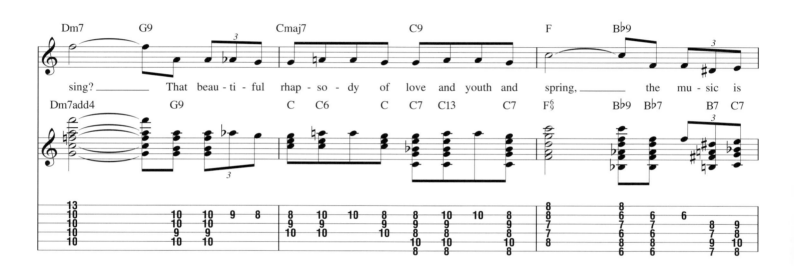

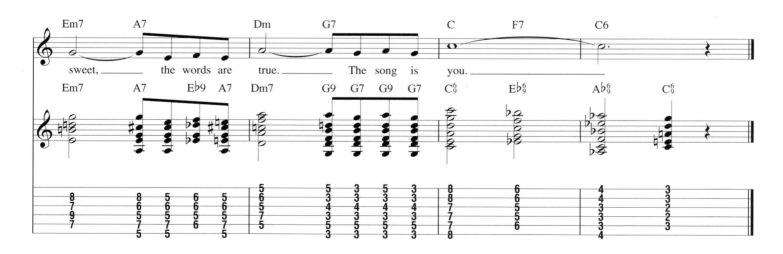

Additional Lyrics

2. I hear music when I touch your hand,
   A beautiful melody from some enchanted land.
   Down deep in my heart, I hear it say, "Is this the day?"

The Way You Look Tonight

Words by Dorothy Fields
Music by Jerome Kern

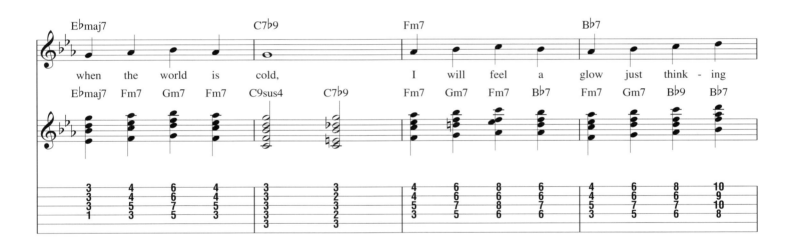

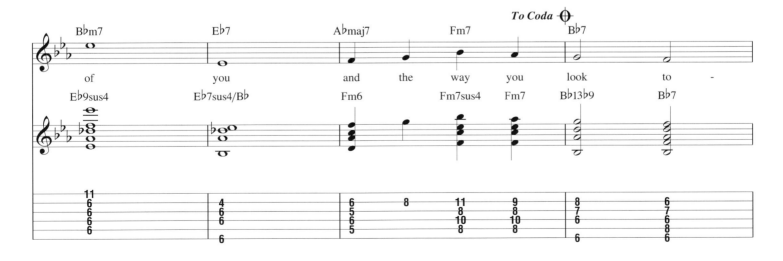

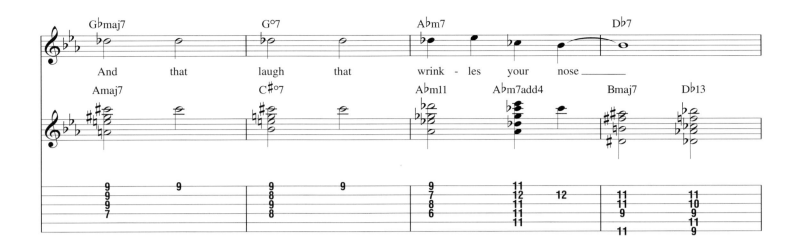

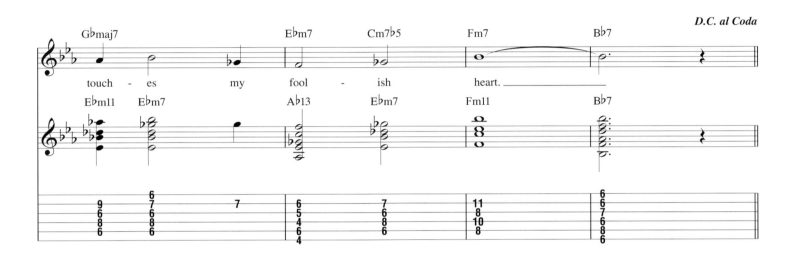

D.C. al Coda

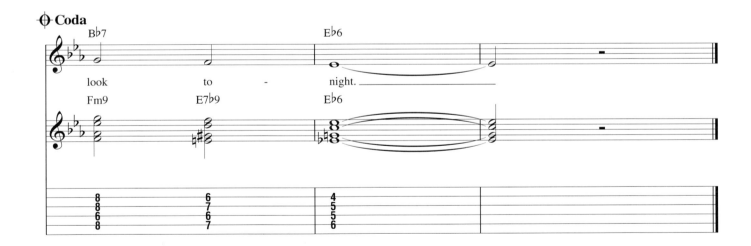

Additional Lyrics

2. Oh, but you're lovely with your smile so warm,
   And your cheeks so soft.
   There is nothing for me but to love you
   Just the way you look tonight.

3. Lovely, never, never change.
   Keep that breathless charm.
   Won't you please arrange it, 'cause I love you
   Just the way you look tonight.

A Sunday Kind of Love

Words and Music by Barbara Belle, Louis Prima, Anita Leonard and Stan Rhodes

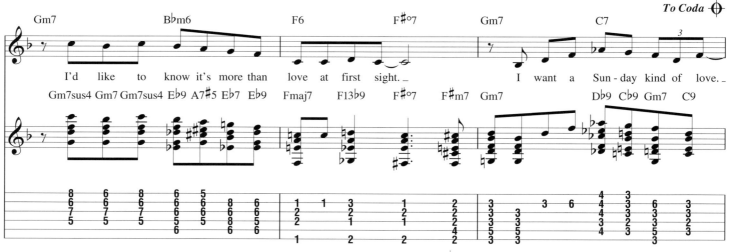

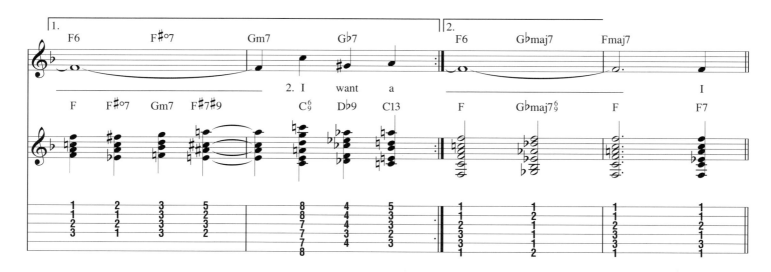

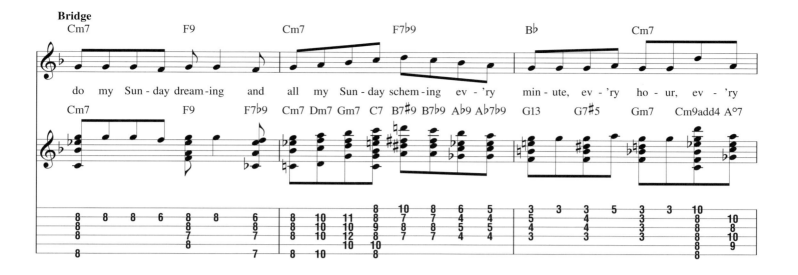

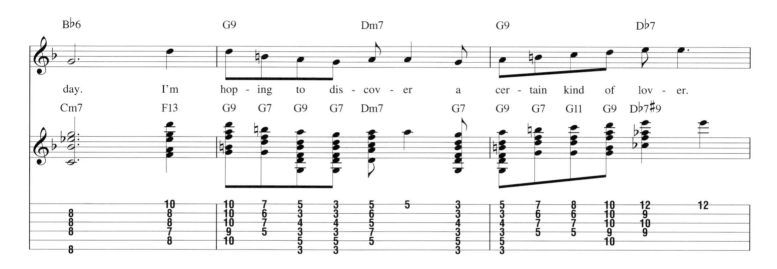

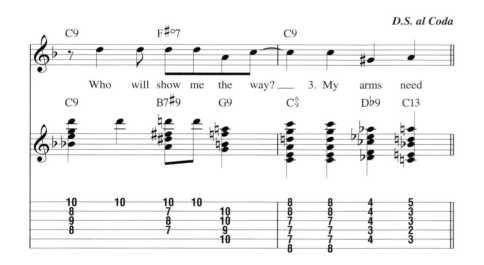

Additional Lyrics

2. I want a love that's on the square.
   Can't seem to find somebody to care.
   I'm on a lonely road that leads me nowhere.
   I need a Sunday kind of love.

3. My arms need someone to enfold
   To keep me warm when Mondays are cold,
   A love for all my life to have and to hold.
   I want a Sunday kind of love.

Watch What Happens

Music by Michel Legrand
Original French Text by Jacques Demy
English Lyrics by Norman Gimbel

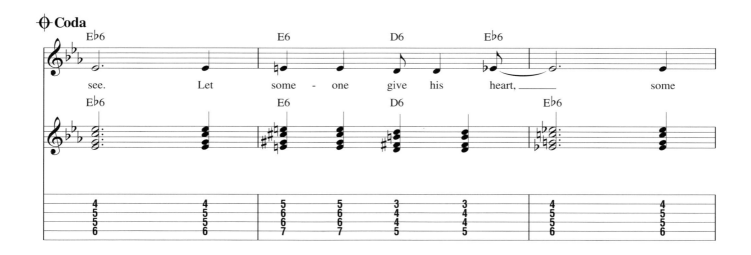

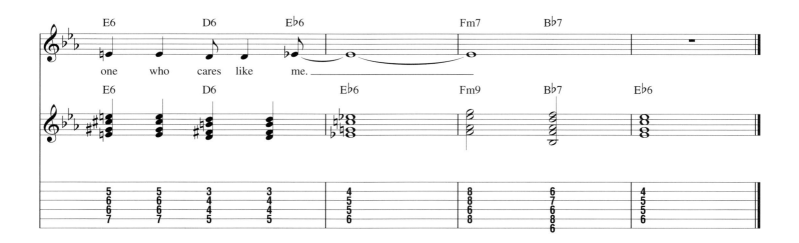

Additional Lyrics

2. One someone who can look in your eyes
   And see into your heart.
   Let him find you and watch what happens.

3. Let someone with a deep love to give
   Give that deep love to you,
   And what magic you will see.
   Let someone give his heart,
   Some one who cares like me.

With a Song in My Heart

Words by Lorenz Hart
Music by Richard Rodgers

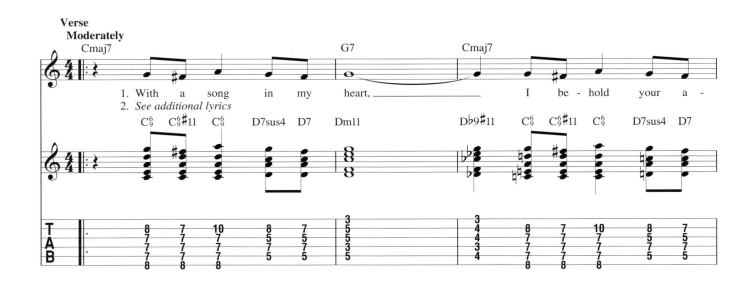

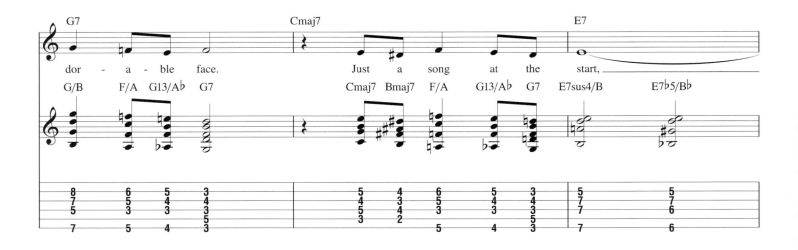

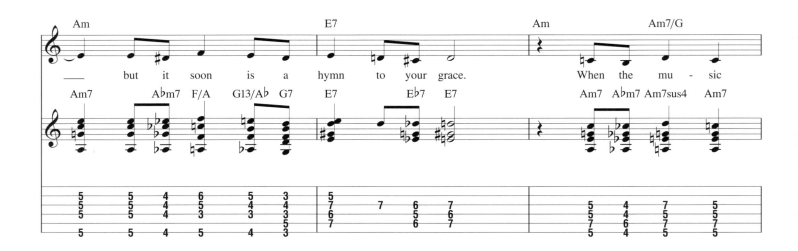

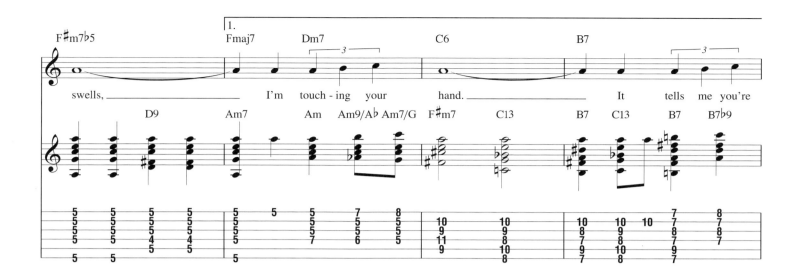

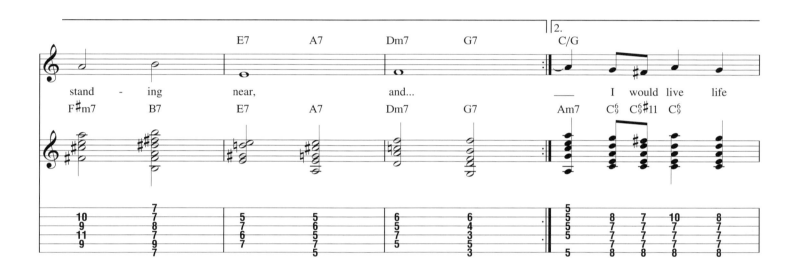

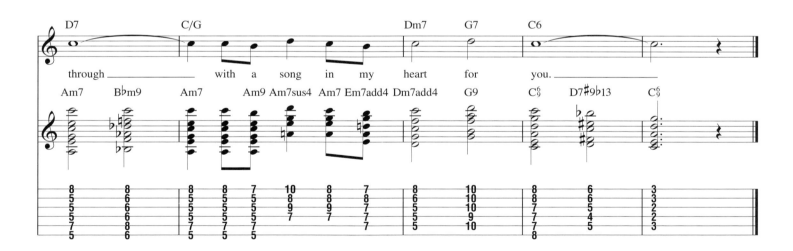

Additional Lyrics

2. At the sound of your voice,
   Heaven opens its portals to me.
   Can I help but rejoice
   That a song such as ours came to be?
   But I always knew I would live life through
   With a song in my heart for you.

Yesterdays

Words by Otto Harbach
Music by Jerome Kern

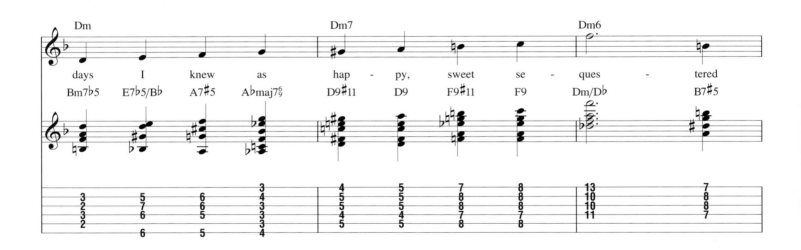

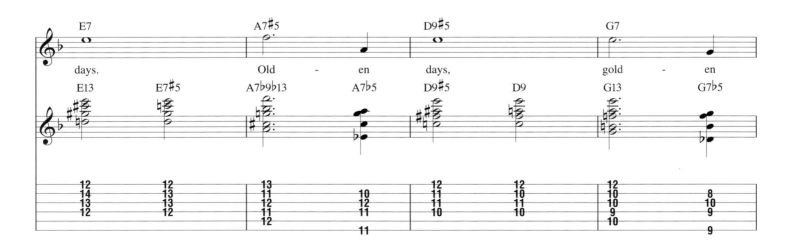

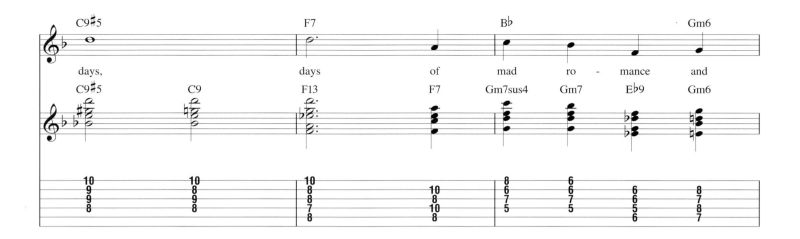

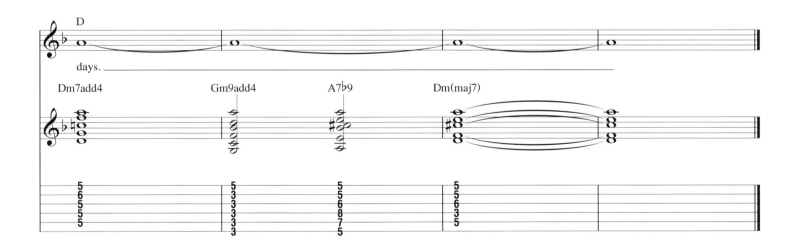

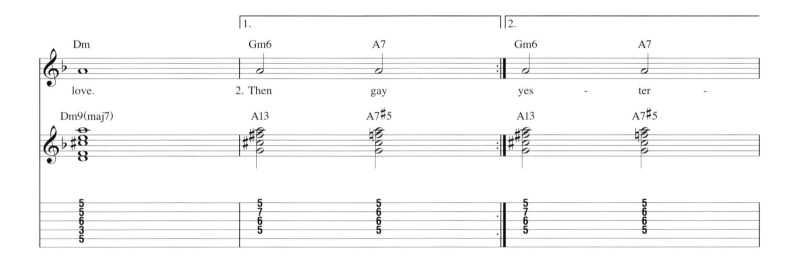

Additional Lyrics

2. Then gay youth was mine, truth was mine.
   Joyous, free and flaming life, forsooth, was mine.
   Sad am I, glad am I, for today I'm dreaming of yesterdays.

You Brought a
New Kind of Love to Me

from the Paramount Picture THE BIG POND

Words and Music by Sammy Fain, Irving Kahal and Pierre Norman

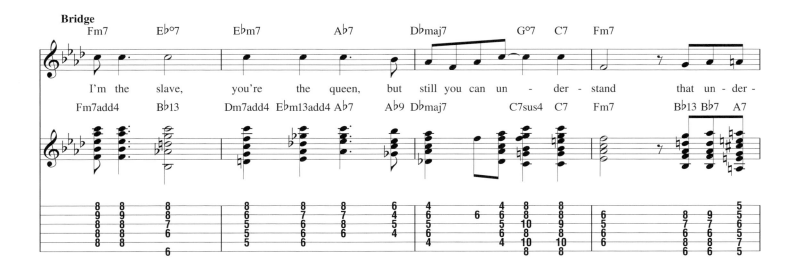

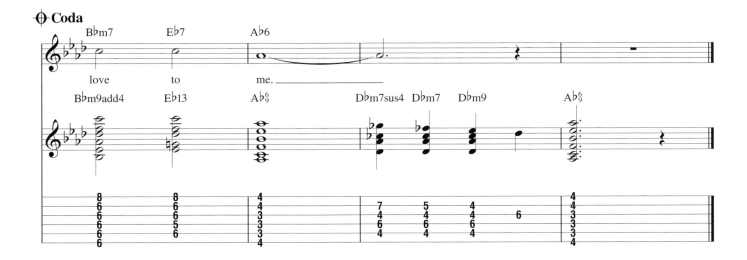

Additional Lyrics

2. If the sandman brought me dreams of you,
   I'd want to sleep my whole life through,
   For you've brought a new kind of love to me.

3. I would work and slave the whole day through
   If I could hurry home to you,
   For you've brought a new kind of love to me.

You Don't Know What Love Is

Words and Music by Don Raye and Gene DePaul

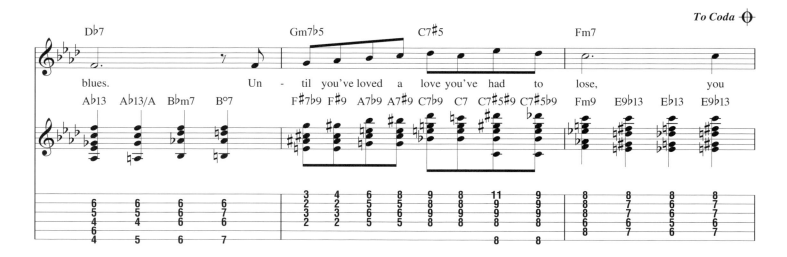

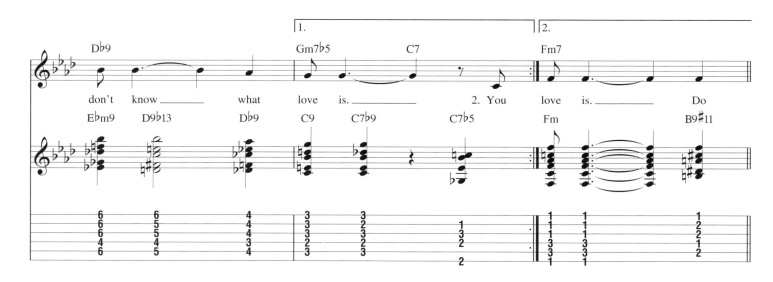

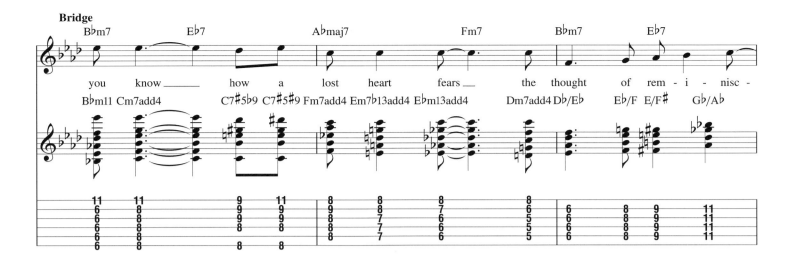

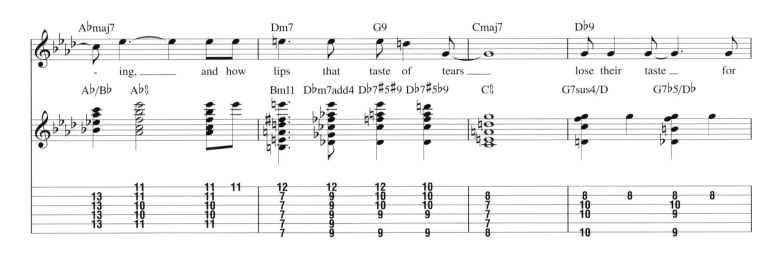

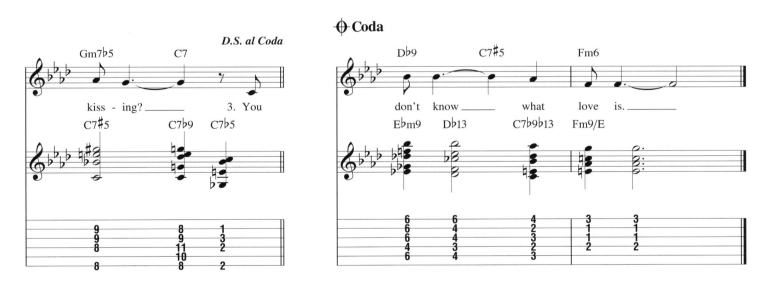

Additional Lyrics

2. You don't know how lips hurt
   Until you've kissed and had to pay the cost.
   Until you've flipped your heart and you have lost,
   You don't know what love is.

3. You don't know how hearts burn
   For love that cannot live, yet never dies.
   Until you've faced each dawn with sleepless eyes,
   You don't know what love is.

ABOUT THE AUTHOR

Robert Yelin is a guitarist, arranger, educator, and writer who has been playing jazz for over 40 years. His first inspiration came from Johnny Smith's chord-melody solos, and it was the rich variety of guitar chords that moved him to arrange nearly 2,000 songs to date. His 1982 album *Night Rain* was named best solo instrumental album in *Cadence* magazine's critics poll. *Guitar Player* wrote: "Yelin's arrangements are unique. He looks for the right chord; not the right lick. He uses alternate tunings, harmonics, and pizzicato effects tastefully while he whips through difficult passages with no sense of strain." In the liner notes for Yelin's jazz trio album *Song For My Wife*, Johnny Smith wrote: "Bob Yelin is an excellent jazz guitarist and this is an excellent album. His music leaves a lasting, musical memory."

In addition to leading the jazz guitar ensemble at the University of Colorado, Bob Yelin has had over 3,500 private students. For more than 20 years he has taught improvisation and chords through his correspondence course. He was *Guitar Player's* contributing jazz editor from 1968-1982, and his writings have also appeared in *Frets* and *Just Jazz Guitar* magazines. His bio can be found in *Who's Who in Entertainment* and the highly respected book, *The Jazz Guitar — It's Evolution, Players and Personalities Since 1900*. He has performed throughout the United States as a solo artist and with his jazz trio.

Fellow jazz great Gene Bertoncini may have put it best when he described Bob Yelin and himself as "chordiologists."

Robert Yelin plays 6, 7, and 14 string Buscarino archtop guitars.

Buscarino Guitars
2348 Wide Horizon Drive
Franklin, N.C. 28734
(828) 349-9867

Guitar Notation Legend

Guitar Music can be notated three different ways: on a *musical staff*, in *tablature*, and in *rhythm slashes*.

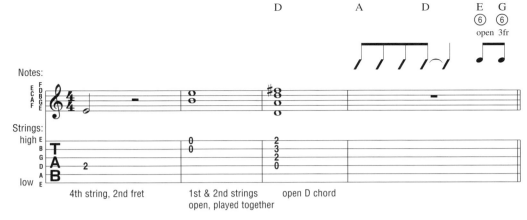

RHYTHM SLASHES are written above the staff. Strum chords in the rhythm indicated. Use the chord diagrams found at the top of the first page of the transcription for the appropriate chord voicings. Round noteheads indicate single notes.

THE MUSICAL STAFF shows pitches and rhythms and is divided by bar lines into measures. Pitches are named after the first seven letters of the alphabet.

TABLATURE graphically represents the guitar fingerboard. Each horizontal line represents a a string, and each number represents a fret.

4th string, 2nd fret

1st & 2nd strings open, played together

open D chord

Definitions for Special Guitar Notation

HALF-STEP BEND: Strike the note and bend up 1/2 step.

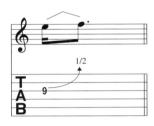

WHOLE-STEP BEND: Strike the note and bend up one step.

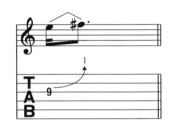

GRACE NOTE BEND: Strike the note and immediately bend up as indicated.

SLIGHT (MICROTONE) BEND: Strike the note and bend up 1/4 step.

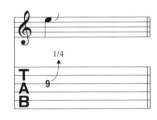

BEND AND RELEASE: Strike the note and bend up as indicated, then release back to the original note. Only the first note is struck.

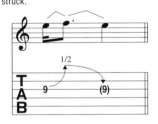

PRE-BEND: Bend the note as indicated, then strike it.

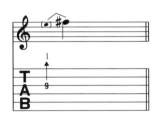

PRE-BEND AND RELEASE: Bend the note as indicated. Strike it and release the bend back to the original note.

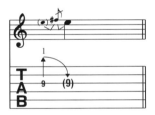

UNISON BEND: Strike the two notes simultaneously and bend the lower note up to the pitch of the higher.

VIBRATO: The string is vibrated by rapidly bending and releasing the note with the fretting hand.

WIDE VIBRATO: The pitch is varied to a greater degree by vibrating with the fretting hand.

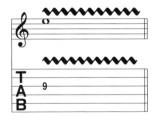

HAMMER-ON: Strike the first (lower) note with one finger, then sound the higher note (on the same string) with another finger by fretting it without picking.

PULL-OFF: Place both fingers on the notes to be sounded. Strike the first note and without picking, pull the finger off to sound the second (lower) note.

LEGATO SLIDE: Strike the first note and then slide the same fret-hand finger up or down to the second note. The second note is not struck.

SHIFT SLIDE: Same as legato slide, except the second note is struck.

TRILL: Very rapidly alternate between the notes indicated by continuously hammering on and pulling off.

TAPPING: Hammer ("tap") the fret indicated with the pick-hand index or middle finger and pull off to the note fretted by the fret hand.

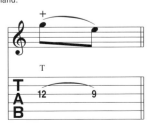

85

NATURAL HARMONIC: Strike the note while the fret-hand lightly touches the string directly over the fret indicated.

Harm.

PINCH HARMONIC: The note is fretted normally and a harmonic is produced by adding the edge of the thumb or the tip of the index finger of the pick hand to the normal pick attack.

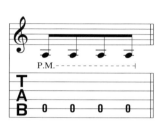

P.H.

HARP HARMONIC: The note is fretted normally and a harmonic is produced by gently resting the pick hand's index finger directly above the indicated fret (in parentheses) while the pick hand's thumb or pick assists by plucking the appropriate string.

H.H.

PICK SCRAPE: The edge of the pick is rubbed down (or up) the string, producing a scratchy sound.

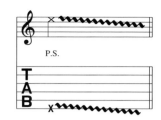

P.S.

MUFFLED STRINGS: A percussive sound is produced by laying the fret hand across the string(s) without depressing, and striking them with the pick hand.

PALM MUTING: The note is partially muted by the pick hand lightly touching the string(s) just before the bridge.

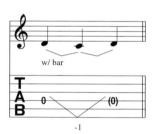

P.M.

RAKE: Drag the pick across the strings indicated with a single motion.

rake

TREMOLO PICKING: The note is picked as rapidly and continuously as possible.

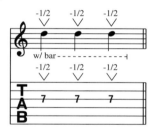

ARPEGGIATE: Play the notes of the chord indicated by quickly rolling them from bottom to top.

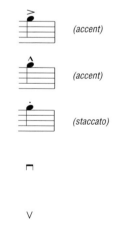

VIBRATO BAR DIVE AND RETURN: The pitch of the note or chord is dropped a specified number of steps (in rhythm) then returned to the original pitch.

w/ bar

VIBRATO BAR SCOOP: Depress the bar just before striking the note, then quickly release the bar.

w/ bar

VIBRATO BAR DIP: Strike the note and then immediately drop a specified number of steps, then release back to the original pitch.

w/ bar

Additional Musical Definitions

(accent)	• Accentuate note (play it louder)	
(accent)	• Accentuate note with great intensity	
(staccato)	• Play the note short	
	• Downstroke	
V	• Upstroke	

D.S. al Coda
• Go back to the sign (𝄋), then play until the measure marked "**To Coda**," then skip to the section labelled "**Coda**."

D.C. al Fine
• Go back to the beginning of the song and play until the measure marked "**Fine**" (end).

Rhy. Fig.
• Label used to recall a recurring accompaniment pattern (usually chordal).

Riff
• Label used to recall composed, melodic lines (usually single notes) which recur.

Fill
• Label used to identify a brief melodic figure which is to be inserted into the arrangement.

Rhy. Fill
• A chordal version of a Fill.

tacet
• Instrument is silent (drops out).

• Repeat measures between signs.

1. ‖ 2.
• When a repeated section has different endings, play the first ending only the first time and the second ending only the second time.

NOTE: Tablature numbers in parentheses mean:
1. The note is being sustained over a system (note in standard notation is tied), or
2. The note is sustained, but a new articulation (such as a hammer-on, pull-off, slide or vibrato begins), or
3. The note is a barely audible "ghost" note (note in standard notation is also in parentheses).

HAL•LEONARD GUITAR PLAY-ALONG®

This series will help you play your favorite songs quickly and easily. Just follow the tab and listen to the CD to hear how the guitar should sound, and then play along using the separate backing tracks. Mac or PC users can also slow down the tempo without changing pitch by using the CD in their computer. The melody and lyrics are included in the book so that you can sing or simply follow along.

INCLUDES TAB

VOL. 1 – ROCK GUITAR 00699570 / $14.95
Day Tripper • Message in a Bottle • Refugee • Shattered • Sunshine of Your Love • Takin' Care of Business • Tush • Walk This Way.

VOL. 2 – ACOUSTIC 00699569 / $14.95
Angie • Behind Blue Eyes • Best of My Love • Blackbird • Dust in the Wind • Layla • Night Moves • Yesterday.

VOL. 3 – HARD ROCK 00699573 / $14.95
Crazy Train • Iron Man • Living After Midnight • Rock You like a Hurricane • Round and Round • Smoke on the Water • Sweet Child O' Mine • You Really Got Me.

VOL. 4 – POP/ROCK 00699571 / $14.95
Breakdown • Crazy Little Thing Called Love • Hit Me with Your Best Shot • I Want You to Want Me • Lights • R.O.C.K. in the U.S.A. • Summer of '69 • What I Like About You.

VOL. 5 – MODERN ROCK 00699574 / $14.95
Aerials • Alive • Bother • Chop Suey! • Control • Last Resort • Take a Look Around (Theme from M:I-2) • Wish You Were Here.

VOL. 6 – '90S ROCK 00699572 / $14.95
Are You Gonna Go My Way • Come Out and Play • I'll Stick Around • Know Your Enemy • Man in the Box • Outshined • Smells Like Teen Spirit • Under the Bridge.

VOL. 7 – BLUES GUITAR 00699575 / $14.95
All Your Love (I Miss Loving) • Born Under a Bad Sign • Hide Away • I'm Tore Down • I'm Your Hoochie Coochie Man • Pride and Joy • Sweet Home Chicago • The Thrill Is Gone.

VOL. 8 – ROCK 00699585 / $14.95
All Right Now • Black Magic Woman • Get Back • Hey Joe • Layla • Love Me Two Times • Won't Get Fooled Again • You Really Got Me.

VOL. 9 – PUNK ROCK 00699576 / $14.95
All the Small Things • Fat Lip • Flavor of the Weak • I Feel So • Lifestyles of the Rich and Famous• Say It Ain't So • Self Esteem • (So) Tired of Waiting for You.

VOL. 10 – ACOUSTIC 00699586 / $14.95
Here Comes the Sun • Landslide • The Magic Bus • Norwegian Wood (This Bird Has Flown) • Pink Houses • Space Oddity • Tangled Up in Blue • Tears in Heaven.

VOL. 11 – EARLY ROCK 00699579 / $14.95
Fun, Fun, Fun • Hound Dog • Louie, Louie • No Particular Place to Go • Oh, Pretty Woman • Rock Around the Clock • Under the Boardwalk • Wild Thing.

VOL. 12 – POP/ROCK 00699587 / $14.95
867-5309/Jenny • Every Breath You Take • Money for Nothing • Rebel, Rebel • Run to You • Ticket to Ride • Wonderful Tonight • You Give Love a Bad Name.

VOL. 13 – FOLK ROCK 00699581 / $14.95
Annie's Song • Leaving on a Jet Plane • Suite: Judy Blue Eyes • This Land Is Your Land • Time in a Bottle • Turn! Turn! Turn! • You've Got a Friend • You've Got to Hide Your Love Away.

VOL. 14 – BLUES ROCK 00699582 / $14.95
Blue on Black • Crossfire • Cross Road Blues (Crossroads) • The House Is Rockin' • La Grange • Move It on Over • Roadhouse Blues • Statesboro Blues.

VOL. 15 – R&B 00699583 / $14.95
Ain't Too Proud to Beg • Brick House • Get Ready • I Can't Help Myself • I Got You (I Feel Good) • I Heard It Through the Grapevine • My Girl • Shining Star.

VOL. 16 – JAZZ 00699584 / $14.95
All Blues • Bluesette • Footprints • How Insensitive • Misty • Satin Doll • Stella by Starlight • Tenor Madness.

VOL. 17 – COUNTRY 00699588 / $14.95
Amie • Boot Scootin' Boogie • Chattahoochee • Folsom Prison Blues • Friends in Low Places • Forever and Ever, Amen • T-R-O-U-B-L-E • Workin' Man Blues.

VOL. 18 – ACOUSTIC ROCK 00699577 / $14.95
About a Girl • Breaking the Girl • Drive • Iris • More Than Words • Patience • Silent Lucidity • 3 AM.

VOL. 19 – SOUL 00699578 / $14.95
Get Up (I Feel Like Being) a Sex Machine • Green Onions • In the Midnight Hour • Knock on Wood • Mustang Sally • Respect • (Sittin' On) the Dock of the Bay • Soul Man.

VOL. 20 – ROCKABILLY 00699580 / $14.95
Be-Bop-A-Lula • Blue Suede Shoes • Hello Mary Lou • Little Sister • Mystery Train • Rock This Town • Stray Cat Strut • That'll Be the Day.

VOL. 21 – YULETIDE 00699602 / $14.95
Angels We Have Heard on High • Away in a Manger • Deck the Hall • The First Noel • Go, Tell It on the Mountain • Jingle Bells • Joy to the World • O Little Town of Bethlehem.

VOL. 22 – CHRISTMAS 00699600 / $14.95
The Christmas Song • Frosty the Snow Man • Happy Xmas • Here Comes Santa Claus • Jingle-Bell Rock • Merry Christmas, Darling • Rudolph the Red-Nosed Reindeer • Silver Bells.

VOL. 23 – SURF 00699635 / $14.95
Let's Go Trippin' • Out of Limits • Penetration • Pipeline • Surf City • Surfin' U.S.A. • Walk Don't Run • The Wedge.

VOL. 24 – ERIC CLAPTON 00699649 / $14.95
Badge • Bell Bottom Blues • Change the World • Cocaine • Key to the Highway • Lay Down Sally • White Room • Wonderful Tonight.

VOL. 25 – LENNON & McCARTNEY 00699642 / $14.95
Back in the U.S.S.R. • Drive My Car • Get Back • A Hard Day's Night • I Feel Fine • Paperback Writer • Revolution • Ticket to Ride.

VOL. 26 – ELVIS PRESLEY 00699643 / $14.95
All Shook Up • Blue Suede Shoes • Don't Be Cruel • Heartbreak Hotel • Hound Dog • Jailhouse Rock • Little Sister • Mystery Train.

VOL. 27 – DAVID LEE ROTH 00699645 / $14.95
Ain't Talkin' 'Bout Love • Dance the Night Away • Hot for Teacher • Just Like Paradise • A Lil' Ain't Enough • Runnin' with the Devil • Unchained • Yankee Rose.

VOL. 28 – GREG KOCH 00699646 / $14.95
Chief's Blues • Death of a Bassman • Dylan the Villain • The Grip • Holy Grail • Spank It • Tonus Diabolicus • Zoiks.

VOL. 29 – BOB SEGER 00699647 / $14.95
Against the Wind • Betty Lou's Gettin' Out Tonight • Hollywood Nights • Mainstreet • Night Moves • Old Time Rock & Roll • Rock and Roll Never Forgets • Still the Same.

VOL. 30 – KISS 00699644 / $14.95
Cold Gin • Detroit Rock City • Deuce • Firehouse • Heaven's on Fire • Love Gun • Rock and Roll All Nite • Shock Me.

VOL. 31 – CHRISTMAS HITS 00699652 / $14.95
Blue Christmas • Do You Hear What I Hear • Happy Holiday • I Saw Mommy Kissing Santa Claus • I'll Be Home for Christmas • Let It Snow! Let It Snow! Let It Snow! • Little Saint Nick • Snowfall.

VOL. 32 – THE OFFSPRING 00699653 / $14.95
Bad Habit • Come Out and Play • Gone Away • Gotta Get Away • Hit That • The Kids Aren't Alright • Pretty Fly (For a White Guy) • Self Esteem.

VOL. 33 – ACOUSTIC CLASSICS 00699656 / $14.95
Across the Universe • Babe, I'm Gonna Leave You • Crazy on You • Heart of Gold • Hotel California • I'd Love to Change the World • Thick As a Brick • Wanted Dead or Alive.

VOL. 34 – CLASSIC ROCK 00699658 / $14.95
Aqualung • Born to Be Wild • The Boys Are Back in Town • Brown Eyed Girl • Reeling in the Years • Rock'n Me • Rocky Mountain Way • Sweet Emotion.

VOL. 35 – HAIR METAL 00699660 / $14.95
Decadence Dance • Don't Treat Me Bad • Down Boys • Seventeen • Shake Me • Up All Night • Wait • Talk Dirty to Me.

VOL. 36 – SOUTHERN ROCK 00699661 / $14.95
Can't You See • Flirtin' with Disaster • Hold on Loosely • Jessica • Mississippi Queen • Ramblin' Man • Sweet Home Alabama • What's Your Name.

VOL. 37 – ACOUSTIC METAL 00699662 / $14.95
Every Rose Has Its Thorn • Fly to the Angels • Hole Hearted • Love Is on the Way • Love of a Lifetime • Signs • To Be with You • When the Children Cry.

VOL. 38 – BLUES 00699663 / $14.95
Boom Boom • Cold Shot • Crosscut Saw • Everyday I Have the Blues • Frosty • Further On up the Road • Killing Floor • Texas Flood.

VOL. 39 – '80S METAL 00699664 / $14.95
Bark at the Moon • Big City Nights • Breaking the Chains • Cult of Personality • Lay It Down • Living on a Prayer • Panama • Smokin' in the Boys Room.

VOL. 40 – INCUBUS 00699668 / $14.95
Are You In? • Drive • Megalomaniac • Nice to Know You • Pardon Me • Stellar • Talk Shows on Mute • Wish You Were Here.

VOL. 41 – ERIC CLAPTON 00699669 / $14.95
After Midnight • Can't Find My Way Home • Forever Man • I Shot the Sheriff • I'm Tore Down • Pretending • Running on Faith • Tears in Heaven.

VOL. 42 – CHART HITS 00699670 / $14.95
Are You Gonna Be My Girl • Heaven • Here Without You • I Believe in a Thing Called Love • Just Like You • Last Train Home • This Love • Until the Day I Die.

VOL. 43 – LYNYRD SKYNYRD 00699681 / $14.95
Don't Ask Me No Questions • Free Bird • Gimme Three Steps • I Know a Little • Saturday Night Special • Sweet Home Alabama • That Smell • You Got That Right.

VOL. 44 – JAZZ 00699689 / $14.95
I Remember You • I'll Remember April • Impressions • In a Mellow Tone • Moonlight in Vermont • On a Slow Boat to China • Things Ain't What They Used to Be • Yesterdays.

VOL. 46 – MAINSTREAM ROCK 00699722 / $14.95
Just a Girl • Keep Away • Kryptonite • Lightning Crashes • 1979 • One Step Closer • Scar Tissue • Torn.

VOL. 47 – HENDRIX SMASH HITS 00699723/ $16.95
All Along the Watchtower • Can You See Me? • Crosstown Traffic • Fire • Foxey Lady • Hey Joe • Manic Depression • Purple Haze • Red House • Remember • Stone Free • The Wind Cries Mary.

VOL. 48 – AEROSMITH CLASSICS 00699724 / $14.95
Back in the Saddle • Draw the Line • Dream On • Last Child • Mama Kin • Same Old Song & Dance • Sweet Emotion • Walk This Way.

VOL. 50 – NÜ METAL 00699726 / $14.95
Duality • Here to Stay • In the End • Judith • Nookie • So Cold • Toxicity • Whatever.

VOL. 51 – ALTERNATIVE '90S 00699727 / $14.95
Alive • Cherub Rock • Come As You Are • Give It Away • Jane Says • No Excuses • No Rain • Santeria.

VOL. 56 – FOO FIGHTERS 00699749 / $14.95
All My Life • Best of You • DOA • I'll Stick Around • Learn to Fly • Monkey Wrench • My Hero • This Is a Call.

VOL. 57 – SYSTEM OF A DOWN 00699751 / $14.95
Aerials • B.Y.O.B. • Chop Suey! • Innervision • Question! • Spiders • Sugar • Toxicity.

Prices, contents, and availability subject to change without notice.

FOR MORE INFORMATION, SEE YOUR LOCAL MUSIC DEALER, OR WRITE TO:

HAL•LEONARD® CORPORATION
7777 W. BLUEMOUND RD. P.O. BOX 13819 MILWAUKEE, WI 53213

Visit Hal Leonard online at www.halleonard.com

0106